101 TROPES YOU SHOULD KNOW

C. BROWN

101 Tropes You Should Know

What Tropes Are, and How We Use Them

by C.Brown

Published by TLM Publishing House

5905 Atlanta Highway, Alpharetta GA.

https://www.ttpublishinghouse.com

Introduction

Welcome to the world of tropes, characters, plots and storytelling. If you have a world stuck in that head of yours, this is one of the steps you need to get through in order to get that story on paper.

Issue there is, many people don't even know what a trope is, and fewer know all of the ways you can utilize them for plotting, character-building, and world-building.

That's where this guide comes in. We've put together 101 Fictional Tropes You Should Know, What Tropes Are, and How We Use Them. Whether you're a beginner, a seasoned pro, or building characters for a tabletop roleplaying game, this guide is designed to give you the knowledge and confidence you need to take your writing to the next level.

Now, you might be thinking, "What are tropes? Aren't they cliche? Can't I just wing it and hope for the best?" You can't necessarily "wing" writing because even pantsers have a rough idea of where they're going with the story. You need to build your characters, and your setting before you dive into the planning (outlining, drafting, going back and changing details to line up with later information, etc) or pantsing (going crazy with writing, while referring to your built characters/setting and letting your imagination run wild.

So, if you want to build characters and worlds for your stories, film projects, or tabletop RPG campaign? This book is your quick reference guide for different tropes, how to use them, and how to predict the ending of every movie you watch from this point on.

II

Contents

What are Tropes?: 1
What a Trope isn't: 1
How Tropes work: 2
The Hero: 3
The Villain: 4
The Big Good: 5
The Big Bad: 6
The Dragon: 7
The Mentor: 8
The Journey: 9
Downer ending: 10
Bittersweet Ending: 11
Bolivian Army Ending: 12
Cliffhanger: 13
The End: 14
Sequel Hook: 15
The War: 16
The Resistance: 17
The Empire: 18
Complete Monster: 19
Black Comedy: 20
The Stoic: 21
The Determinator: 22
Ax Crazy: 23

The Hero Dies: 24
Curb-Stomp Battle: 25
11th-Hour Superpower: 26
Story-Breaker Superpower: 27
Everyman: 28
Fish out of Water: 29
Fish out of Temporal Water: 30
Trapped in Another World: 31
Running Gag: 32
Brick Joke: 33
Heroic Sacrifice: 34
Foreshadowing: 35
Exactly What It Says on the Tin: 36
Character Development: 37
Large Ham: 38
Suspension of Disbelief: 39
Rule of Cool: 40
Catchphrase: 41
Action Girl: 42
The Reveal: 43
Pet the Dog: 44
Only Sane Man: 45
Too Dumb to Live: 46
The Load: 47
Noodle Incident: 48
Even Evil has Standards: 49

Nice Job Breaking It, Hero: 50
Chekhov's Gun: 51
Blood Knight: 52
Karma Houdini: 53
Face-Heel Turn: 54
The Dreaded: 55
One-Man Army: 56
Mooks: 57
Mook Horror Show: 58
Beware the Nice Ones: 59
Laser-Guided Karma: 60
O.O.C is Serious Business: 61
Anti-Hero: 62
The Woobie (pronounced wuh-bee): 63
Nice Guy: 64
Evil Counterpart: 65
Affably Evil: 66
Faux-Affably Evil: 67
Hypocrite: 68
And I Must Scream: 69
Moral Event Horizon: 70
Eye Scream: 71
Reasonable Authority Figure: 72
Establishing Character Moment: 73
Truth in Television: 74
Arch-Enemy: 75

Despair Event Horizon: 76
The Mole: 77
Papa Wolf: 78
Mama Bear: 79
Killed Off for Real: 80
Death is Cheap: 81
The Chessmaster: 82
Smug Snake: 83
Comically Missing the Point: 84
The Ace: 85
Roaring Rampage of Revenge: 86
Bad Boss: 87
Sanity Slippage: 88
Ascended Extra: 89
No-Sell: 90
Undying Loyalty: 91
Wham Episode: 92
Break the Cutie: 93
The Atoner: 94
Put on a Bus: 95
The Bus Came Back: 96
Book Ends: 97
Groin Attack: 98
Punny Name: 99
Never My Fault: 100
Breaking the Fourth Wall: 101

True Companions: 102
Must Have Caffeine: 103
More From TLM Publishing: 104

What Are Tropes?

A trope is a plot device, used to add depth, function and originality into a work of fiction. Tropes are seen all around in books, films, television shows and animation, but you can even see them apply in real life if you look carefully enough.

Due to how broad of a definition the word "trope" is, it can be hard to pinpoint exactly when a trope begins, and when it ends, but the simple answer to the question "is X a trope?" is almost always going to be a "yes;" here's why.

Stories revolve around plotlines. These plotlines run off of arcs and plot devices (herein referred to as a trope.) Every story has a plotline, and within these plotlines, you will see characters at their best, at their worst, and fighting to get what they want.

Characters within a story should feel human, no matter the setting, so tropes are utilized to give them depth, a motive to take on the main plotline, and the various traits that help or hinder them throughout.

Now onto what a trope *isn't*.

A trope isn't a stereotype. A stereotype is a trope that has been used so frequently that it's practically an expectation amongst certain genres.

A trope isn't going to solve every roadblock you run into with writing. Tropes are tools, and just like tools, you need to utilize them properly.

Practice with tropes and building characters, ask your friends and family if they seem to have any depth and test out how different tropes interact with each other, like you're experimenting with chemistry. Have fun with it, and try to spot tropes in your favorite media to get an idea on how they're used.

How Tropes Work

Play it Straight: The trope is used in the most straightforward manner, and describes how the trope is used in most cases.

Downplayed: The trope is used in a lesser, or weaker extent.

Exaggerated: The trope is played to extremes, amplifying the trope's usage twofold.

Subverted: The trope is built up to, but never fully comes into play.

Zig-Zag: After subverting, you can play it straight after. Playing it straight is double-subverting, whereas subverting afterwards is zig-zagging.

Deconstructed: The trope is broken down and played realistically, with characters reacting appropriately to it.

Reconstructed: After deconstruction, the trope is then played straight, in a realistic manner akin to deconstructions.

Averted: The trope doesn't come into play, or is teased very slightly before being denied.

Lampshading: A character in-universe mentioning the trope in play, whether aware of the fourth wall or not.

Invoked: A character in the story attempting to set a trope into motion, whether consciously or not.

The Hero

Play it Straight	The character acts on the behalf of friends, nations or the greater good and is recognized for their efforts.
Downplayed	The character is a hero, but hardly recognized as such, or performs heroic acts off and on, but doesn't quite make the cut like an "official" hero.
Exaggerated	The character is a pure paragon of unrivaled proportions, pulling off mythical feats to smite down evil and save everyone. Even their own enemies see them as the hero, and they radiate goodness.
Subverted	Someone appears to be a hero, only to do horrible acts on a regular basis. Propaganda or mind control may cause someone particularly nasty to appear as a hero.
Zig-Zag	The character appears to be a hero, but ends up slaughtering an innocent bystander, but that bystander was an enemy spy, but the hero feels remorseless, but deep within he still feels bad for killing someone…
Deconstructed	The hero ends up sustaining psychological trauma from the various atrocities that they've seen and the enemies they've felled, causing them to end up as a jaded, bitter person.
Reconstructed	But despite the above, they still persist and fight the opposition to ensure that no one else has to go through the pain that they have, as a true hero would.
Averted	No one in the setting is deemed a hero, or acts heroic. This may be due to no one being good, the setting or society lacking morals or simply the concept of "heroes" being too far-fetched in-universe.
Lampshading	"Wow, they stopped the admiral's nukes to prevent a third world war, saved everyone from a burning orphanage and donate to charity. What a hero, huh?"
Invoked	A character or group decides that the world or nation needs to have a common figure to rally behind, so they create situations that need a hero in hopes that someone will step in.

The Villain

Play it Straight The character has government officials under their hand, plans on dominating the world and has the power to back it up.

Downplayed A character does acts of villainy out of necessity, whether for survival or their own organization's wellbeing. They don't necessarily like what they're doing anymore than anyone else.

Exaggerated The villain commits war crimes every day, shoots their underlings for fun, twirls their mustache with every atrocity and steals money from charity organizations to burn all of it in their fireplace.

Subverted Like the hero example, a character can appear to be a villain, only to have been framed as such by a group, or they end up being a decoy to keep the actual villain safe.

Zig-Zag The villain blows up a building, but it's actually a gang hideout, though he also destroyed countless works of art, but they were actually counterfeits, *but* it turns out that the gangsters' families were with them...

Deconstructed villain's constant scheming, backstabbing and plotting ends up amounting to nothing, and they're quickly shot down by the various people that they've tried to use...

Reconstructed ...Except they didn't go down that easily, and the people that tried to take them down were really on their side all along. Now they can continue their efforts from the shadows with less pressure.

Averted There are no villains, morals or perception of such in the story.

Lampshading "This guy is the CEO of a multi-billion dollar company, has ties to arms dealers and pays people to solve problems for him. *What a villain.*"

Invoked The world is in a cycle of conflict between nations, tribes and/or ideals, and someone decides that the world needs a common threat to unite and stand up against.

The Big Good

Play it Straight This character leads the forces of good and/or the protagonist into action, carrying the weight of their army on their shoulders, or leading their forces to victory through excellent planning and wit.

Downplayed The character isn't all too helpful for much of anything, but when times get desperate, they will put in their best effort to lead the forces of good to victory.

Exaggerated The character is a godly figure who everyone nearly worships, simply mentioning their name raises morale and them entering any conflict immediately resolves it out of sheer awesomeness and/or respect.

Subverted The king/general/leader whose followers see as a paragon and just leader turns out to be a selfish, manipulative schemer in a similar manner to their enemy.

Zig-Zag The Big Good treats their men well, but they end up firing a nuclear missile, but it was actually to hit an alien spaceship that no one else noticed, but that "alien spaceship" was going to propose a peace treaty...

Deconstructed The Big Good wins the conflict, and they take over the felled empire/form their own nation, but the power they receive begins to twist their morals, and the power begins to get into their head.

Reconstructed ...But they're snapped out of it, whether by their own willpower or the help of their allies, driving them back on the right path.

Averted No one in the setting leads a large-scale effort for the greater good (or benefit for the masses,) or they are multiple leaders for the heroes and their allies as opposed to one.

Lampshading "So you mean to tell me that this guy has everyone's adoration, solved world hunger and actually cares about every single one of his men??"

Invoked The heroes realize that they're charging in blindly, and employ someone (whether of their own, or someone more qualified that they find along the way) to lead them into victory.

The Big Bad

Play it Straight This character is the overarching antagonist for the setting as a whole, not necessarily the antagonist for the protagonist, but rather the character who kicks off the large scale plot and gets things rolling.

Downplayed The character instigates the plot by nefarious means, but does so for a (delusional or legitimately) reason to try and benefit their own side, as opposed to themselves.

Exaggerated The Big Bad is the root of all evil in the setting, corrupting even the greatest of heroes and destroying civilizations with the flick of a wrist.

Subverted The character is either a mouthpiece for the actual Big Bad, or their goals are actually far more beneficial than what was initially perceived.

Zig-Zag The Big Bad begins a war for their own good, but it turns out they're trying to get enough resources to save a loved one, but that was apparently a front and they're keeping the money, but *that* was also a lie...

Deconstructed The Big Bad ends up pushing everyone away due to their selfish desires and goals, and end up failing to build up any real progress on their conquest...

Reconstructed ...So they end up blackmailing or mind controlling people to work for them, and utilize peer pressure to gather forces for their plans.

Averted There is no Big Bad, and the plot is instigated by a group of evil characters or someone who begins the protagonist's journey without the ire of everyone else.

Lampshading "Well we can't be the bad guys, our enemies wear entirely black uniforms, outnumber us 5 to 1 and their leader is a pale, skeletal creep with extremely ambiguous motives!"

Invoked Like the villain example before, a character could see the various groups of people fighting over trivial matters, and end up taking the mantle of a Big Bad to force everyone into uniting against one foe.

The Dragon

Play it Straight The Big Bad's right-hand man, doing the fighting and acting on their behalf as they scheme and order the rest of their forces. Essentially a "hero unit" for the big bad.

Downplayed This character is the Big Bad/Villain's best pawn, and they're the most reliable asset to use despite not necessarily being a "right hand man."

Exaggerated The Dragon ends up doing everything better than the Big Bad/Villain, making the most successful plans, beating the heroes up and being a nigh-unstoppable juggernaut.

Subverted The Dragon ends up eventually betraying their leader, and either forms their own group or joins the protagonist in the large-scale conflict.

Zig-Zag The Dragon is the Big Bad's right hand man, but he's actually a mole for the Big Good/protagonist, but that was a ruse and he's actually a double agent, but they're actually independent to either side...

Deconstructed The Dragon's trials and tribulations under their leader ends up breaking them down, rendering them less loyal and perhaps even disabled as a result...

Reconstructed ...But after a pep talk from their master or allies, they still persist and learn to fight in spite of their handicaps.

Averted The Big Bad or Villain doesn't need or want a right hand man, and takes care of business by themselves or via their many troops.

Lampshading "I swear, I feel like that guy would make a great babysitter if he wasn't working for the evil emperor."

Invoked The Big Bad/Villain decides that they can't run the army/empire alone, so they decide on a right-hand man to help them pick out advisors, deal with physical matters and verify that their plans will work.

The Mentor

Play it Straight The Mentor teaches the protagonist various topics, ranging from survival skills,. to combat, to morals in order to improve them for the final confrontation with the antagonist/big bad/villain.

Downplayed The character mentors the protagonist very little, often giving advice for the situation at hand instead of guiding them through the journey.

Exaggerated The protagonist ends up prepared for the entire journey, their fight with the antagonist and the rest of their life... after one sitting with the Mentor.

Subverted The Mentor's advice ends up backfiring on the protagonist, or the mentor fails to get any of their lessons into the protagonist's head despite their best efforts.

Zig-Zag The Mentor teaches the protagonist valuable information, but the knowledge ends up being useless, though the protagonist learned through their failure, but they're now unable to use said knowledge...

Deconstructed The Mentor tries to teach other characters how to better themselves, but all of their efforts fall onto deaf ears, and the Mentor gives up on trying as a result...

Reconstructed ...Until the characters use the Mentor's lessons, and succeed through them, spurring the Mentor back into action as a result.

Averted The protagonist and their allies learn everything as they come, or the mentor decides that the group can learn everything on their own.

Lampshading "Seriously, is that guy *always* right or something? I don't get how everything he's told us to do has worked so far.

Invoked After seeing the heroes fail time and time again, they agree to find someone to guide them, or another character steps in after seeing the group's numerous failures.

The Journey

Play it Straight The journey that the protagonist and their group goes through for the duration of the story, from saving a town and making friends to taking down the empire.

Downplayed The journey in question is pretty much a short trip or vacation of sorts for the characters, and doesn't really prompt any changes to the status quo.

Exaggerated The journey bears the weight of the multiverse, and if the protagonist and their allies fail, reality ceases to exist.

Subverted The protagonist's crew embarks on a journey, but midway through they're stranded with no real way to continue it.

Zig-Zag The characters embark on a journey, but just as they do, the problem is solved, but they decide to go and travel to other towns and nations anyway, but just before they manage to, one of them falls ill...

Deconstructed The main ensemble goes on a journey, but they end up having no impact on the large scale conflict and lose more than they got...

Reconstructed ...But despite that, they still walk out having learned more about themselves and the world, cherishing the ups of the journey while improving with the downs.

Averted It appears that a grand journey is about to be undertaken by the protagonist, but it turns out that the problem is resolved before they get the chance to.

Lampshading "Didn't you say you were going to the shopping center? Why do you look like you underwent an entire cross-country journey?"

Invoked The protagonist is thrown into a journey outside of their own will by friends, family or outside circumstances, and need to adapt on the fly as a result.

Downer ending

Play it Straight	The heroes are defeated, and maybe even dead as the villains succeed in their plans. There may be a chance to come back from the loss, but more often than not, it's *over.*
Downplayed	The heroes lose, the empire has taken over and the antagonist laughs as the story comes to a close, but the heroes will most likely make a comeback and undo the villains' victory in the next installment.
Exaggerated	The entire universe is destroyed, everyone good and evil has died miserably and the chances for a sequel are flat-out nonexistent.
Subverted	The sidekick is in the villain's grasp, the hero is on their last leg and their allies are nowhere to be found, when one of them suddenly swipes the sidekick out of the villain's grasp and strikes them down.
Zig-Zag	The villains are about to win, and the forces of good are struggling to keep up, but they land a crippling blow on the empire, but the dragon suddenly wipes out half a planet, but the hero kills the dragon...
Deconstructed	The outcome demolishes the morale of the villain's forces, making them rebel against their superiors in hopes that the heroes' sacrifices will not have been in vain.
Reconstructed	...But the villains saw it coming and easily snuffed out the resistance within their own ranks, bringing forth the end as planned.
Averted	The story has a good ending, simply doesn't end as long as the audience is willing to keep watching/ reading/playing or the heroes still have enough power to strike back at a later time.
Lampshading	"So everyone good has died, the status quo is completely unchanged and the villains are now converting orphans into slaves? Who thought this was a good ending?!"
Invoked	The heroes decide that they need to fail, whether to keep the forces of evil off of their tracks or to ensure that no one else gets hurt any longer,

Bittersweet Ending

Play it Straight	The heroes have won, but they've lost a lot of people dear to them and the world(s) have been forever changed by the events of the story.
Downplayed	The heroes have definitely won, but their success isn't without its downsides, and the scars they've made along the way.
Exaggerated	The heroes and villains have both undergone crushing defeats, no side really feels good about it and they all take time to recover from the conflict.
Subverted	Things appear to be coming to a stop, with both sides on their last legs, but one proceeds to evade and the story continues on.
Zig-Zag	The heroes have won, but the big good has died, only to reveal that they were only unconscious, but shortly after that, the hero falls unconscious from their wounds...
Deconstructed	The protagonist losing their friends causes them to fall off the deep end, despite having taken down the villain and their armies.
Reconstructed	...But a friend snaps them out of their stupor, whether by words or force, causing the protagonist to come to terms with their losses and move on.
Averted	The heroes or villains win without question, while retaining their allies as a result. Alternatively, the story simply doesn't end at this point.
Lampshading	"So your friends are all dead, the empire has fallen and you've lost your arm in the conflict. Look out there, it wasn't all for nothing, was it?"
Invoked	The protagonist's allies sacrifice each other one by one to ensure that the villains are crippled for the protagonist to take down.

Bolivian Army Ending

Play it Straight The protagonist has resolved the main conflict, the main villains are felled and all is well, until suddenly a group of stragglers charge the protagonist. The end.

Downplayed The protagonist has resolved the main conflict, but before they can catch a break, the dragon crawls out from the debris and lunges towards the protagonist. The end.

Exaggerated Once again, the protagonist has resolved the main conflict, and before they even get to say a word, hundreds to thousands of enemies rush towards them. The end.

Subverted A group of enemies charge the protagonist near the end of the story, only for the protagonist's allies to also charge in and beat the enemies up.

Zig-Zag A group of enemies charge the protagonist near the end of the story, only for the protagonist's allies to charge in as well, but even *more* enemies charge in and... yeah, the story's going to end before this fight.

Deconstructed The protagonist notices the approaching hostiles, and noticing that he stands no chance against them, runs away in hopes that he can break the chase or find help before he dies...

Reconstructed ...Until he realizes that he's more than capable of beating them up, which prompts him to lunge at his numerous foes. The end.

Averted The last survivors of the empire rush towards the protagonist, only for the protagonist to beat them in mere seconds, leaving the area to end the story traditionally.

Lampshading "Where did these guys come from? I thought this was supposed to be over right around no-"

Invoked Some of the big bad's forces were sitting back and waiting for the protagonist to let their guard down for the best chance to take them down.

Cliffhanger

Play it Straight	The villain has the protagonist hanging on a ledge, aiming a weapon directly at their head. The story ends on that note, expecting a sequel to reveal what happened afterwards.
Downplayed	The villain has the protagonist hanging on a ledge, aiming a weapon directly at their head, but the protagonist pulls the villain down and manages to climb back up, looking down at the villain. The end.
Exaggerated	The villain and protagonist are both on their last legs, they face each other readying up to fight, before the story suddenly ends.
Subverted	The hero pulls the villain down while dangling from the edge, before climbing up and catching their breath, but then the Dragon walks in, the two face each other and the story ends.
Zig-Zag	The protagonist and the villain face eachother down in the last moments of the story, but the villain is struck down and all seems well, except the dragon arrives to fight the hero, but they go down as well...
Deconstructed	The ensuing cliffhanger leaves the story incomplete, and without the proper writing, characters and world building prior, there ends up not being a sequel/next episode/book...
Reconstructed	...Until the writer/studio decides to make a sequel anyway, whether it's to continue the story and keep readers engaged or simply to finish the story.
Averted	The protagonist takes down the villain while dangling on a ledge, before climbing up and completing their mission/quest. The story ends with everything set in stone as a result.
Lampshading	"Oh come on! Seriously, why do these shows always cut off just before the end?!"
Invoked	The villain is aware of the 4th wall, and intentionally times the hero's desperate last moments with the runtime/word count as a jab towards the audience.

The End

Play it Straight The plot and all (or most) subplots are resolved, everyone goes home and lives their lives happy ever after, a standard ending to a story.

Downplayed The story has ended on a steady note, everyone begins to go home, but something on the ground flutters, prompting a potential sequel.

Exaggerated The villains are beat, the heroes are headed home and there's no chance that problems will arise, *ever*. The story's over, and there won't be any more in this setting.

Subverted The story appears to be ending on a steady note, but the dragon appears at the last second (cliffhanger,) the apocalypse wasn't prevented (downer ending) or the heroes are stranded with nowhere left to go.

Zig-Zag The story appears to ending, but the villain emerges, having faked his demise, but he's immediately defeated afterwards and the story ends shortly after.

Deconstructed While the book/film/series ending in such a tidy manner helps for one-off novels, films and spinoffs, it makes your job a lot harder trying to create a sequel for a story that your audience thought was finished...

Reconstructed ...Sure, you can definitely create another sequel afterwards and explain the new motive as you did with the first entry, but if you fully intend for your series to keep going on, it's better to use sequel hooks.

Averted The heroes have defeated the villains at the end of the story, but a new threat appears shortly after, prompting everyone to prepare for another fight.

Lampshading "Alright, that's a wrap. The only thing we'd need now is some text appearing out of thin air, saying "The End."

Invoked The characters, tired of fighting non-stop, decide that the conflict needs to end, so they stop pulling their punches, drop the morals and charge the empire with all they have, resulting in one side destroying the other.

Sequel Hook

Play it Straight The biggest threat in the story is defeated, the heroes prevail despite some losses and all is well, but one character gets a call that something else is coming, as they look at their front door.

Downplayed The story ends on a high note, everyone takes their leave and all seems to be well, but one of the characters proposes a trip with the rest of the crew, the story ending on that note.

Exaggerated The protagonist is still fighting the villains while running out of resources and stranded alone, and the story comes to an end before the conflict does. See Cliffhanger for more details.

Subverted The next installment is out, and the sequel hook from the previous is seemingly absent or used as a red herring, with the plot venturing elsewhere as a result.

Zig-Zag The biggest threat is resolved, the heroes go home and get rest, but the antagonist survived and is plotting his return, but in the next entry, he's completely absent, only to strike at the second half of the story.

Deconstructed The author or studio wants to start or continue a series, and added a sequel hook to ease into another entry, but they run into the risk of the series falling short of the audience's expectations, garnering no hype.

Reconstructed ...But then again, they can simply release the next installment anyways, or opt for a more subtle sequel hook that could be interpreted as a concrete ending *or* a lead-in for a sequel.

Averted The plot is resolved, and everyone continues their lives as usual. The next installment in the series, if there are any, don't involve the protagonists outside of dialog or being present as side characters.

Lampshading "Well done everyone! Big bad's down for the count, his empire's running for the hills and all's well, surely nothing else will happen, right?"

Invoked The villain faked their death, and proceeds to call one of the main characters, leaving an ambiguous threat in the process as the story ends.

The War

Play it Straight A large scale conflict in the story between two nations, morals or the typical "good & evil" sides, often affecting the setting in various ways.

Downplayed The city or nation that the protagonist is in is undergoing a civil war or rebellion, often roping the protagonist in or prompting them to take their leave.

Exaggerated Every nation is fighting a war, wars start and end every day, and everyone in the setting may as well be a soldier.

Subverted The nation pushes to its people that there's a war underway, but it's a lie for the sake of gathering forces and funding for something else entirely.

Zig-Zag A war is brewing, but at the last minute, the government comes to an agreement with their would-be enemy, but a third party launches an attack to instigate conflict...

Deconstructed The conflict ends up draining every side's resources, damages morale for everyone involved and eventually leads into complete anarchy within the nations themselves.

Reconstructed ...But regardless, they continue fighting on, gaining resources and volunteers from other nations in order to make up for what they've lost, and putting a stop to the riots going on within their own country.

Averted A nation is trying not to go to war with another, and tries everything in order to prevent it. They succeed, and the war is ultimately prevented.

Lampshading "Well I don't know, people are being armed and sent out to die and the economy's a complete wreck. It's almost like a *war* or something is going on at the moment?!"

Invoked Political figures decide that their controversies are gaining too much attention, and intentionally start a civil war/international conflict to distract everyone from it.

The Resistance

Play it Straight A group of characters revolting against the empire, their nation or a normalized aspect of society, whether through peaceful protest or violent riots.

Downplayed A small group of people decide to make a change, but due to their minuscule size, their efforts result in very little changes, if anything.

Exaggerated The resistance is fighting against the empire, as the empire's troops are forming resistances against the empire itself while the empire is resisting against an even larger force...

Subverted The resistance is built up as a force to be reckoned with going against the government, only for them to reveal that they're simply protesting a much more trivial matter.

Zig-Zag The resistance is supposedly trying to uproot the empire, but they're a bunch of harmless protesters, until the facade falls short and their real plans for overthrowing their oppressors comes to light.

Deconstructed The resistance ends up running into issues between being outnumbered, lacking supplies and members of the resistance causing more harm than good amidst their ranks.

Reconstructed ...But they manage to solve said problems through better training, improvisation, communication and better management.

Averted The protagonist is told about a group of resistance fighters, but it's revealed that they were a few stragglers who were shot down seconds after their attempted "uprising."

Lampshading "There's a new group of resistance fighters along the coast. It's the 16th group we've had to deal with this week."

Invoked Tired of the Empire's iron-fisted reign, people begin to rally and form a resistance movement to change their nation, world, or even universe.

The Empire

Play it Straight	An organization or global superpower that attempts to take over and/or control nations or worlds, whether for power, resources or to enforce their own code of ethics and morals across the world/galaxy.
Downplayed	An organization within a nation that takes up arms in an attempt to control parts of, or the entirety of the nation that it resides in.
Exaggerated	The empire 's influence reaches past the universe, their resources are innumerable and they have an iron-fisted grasp on all they claim.
Subverted	The "empire" that's been scaring everyone actually has completely mundane goals, and doesn't kills off rebels or plan world domination.
Zig-Zag	The empire that's been scaring everyone is a totally humanitarian organization, but it's revealed later that it was a front, and they really are trying to take over the world.
Deconstructed	The empire's efforts ends up prompting other nations to retaliate while causing rebellions within their own ranks, and with the odds against them, their failure is almost certain.
Reconstructed	...But they end up eliminating the largest threats, getting their troops' morale back up and taking down rebels immediately, almost ensuring their success if it weren't for the heroes.
Averted	There is no empire, whether due to the setting being disorganized, or soon-to-be empires being destroyed before they gain any traction.
Lampshading	"I think we *may* be the bad guys executing those resistance fighters by firing squad..."
Invoked	The Big Bad/Villain determines that they need more forces, and begins to assemble a global superpower to stand a better chance against the world/galaxy.

Complete Monster

Play it Straight	A completely, utterly irredeemable character who's hated by everyone, both in-universe and even by the audiences.
Downplayed	A character who's the most evil thing in the setting, having very few redeeming factors while otherwise remaining inexcusable.
Exaggerated	The monster literally cannot function without eating babies, destroying universes and torturing people once every hour.
Subverted	The monster is horrible because they feel that they *have* to be, or are forced to be this way, they don't *really* want to, but they still perform the atrocities that a complete monster is known for.
Zig-Zag	The character commits countless atrocities, but they were forced to do so by someone else, though they eventually grow to enjoy the rush of their actions afterwards.
Deconstructed	Due to their actions, the complete monster ends up being pursued and outnumbered by everyone they've wronged, which is a *lot* of people.
Reconstructed	...But despite that, they power through and end up torturing and killing off everyone who went after them, using them as a means to attack their families and friends in the process.
Averted	Everyone in the setting has enough of a moral compass to ensure that they'll have some lines they won't cross.
Lampshading	"So your day starts with eating kittens, going to work blowing up orphanages, having a normal guy's insides for dinner, mailing his wife the leftovers and ends with bathing in her blood?"
Invoked	Someone decides that the world needs a common threat to unite against, and beings to commit atrocity after atrocity to make everyone hate them, and therefor focus their efforts on them.

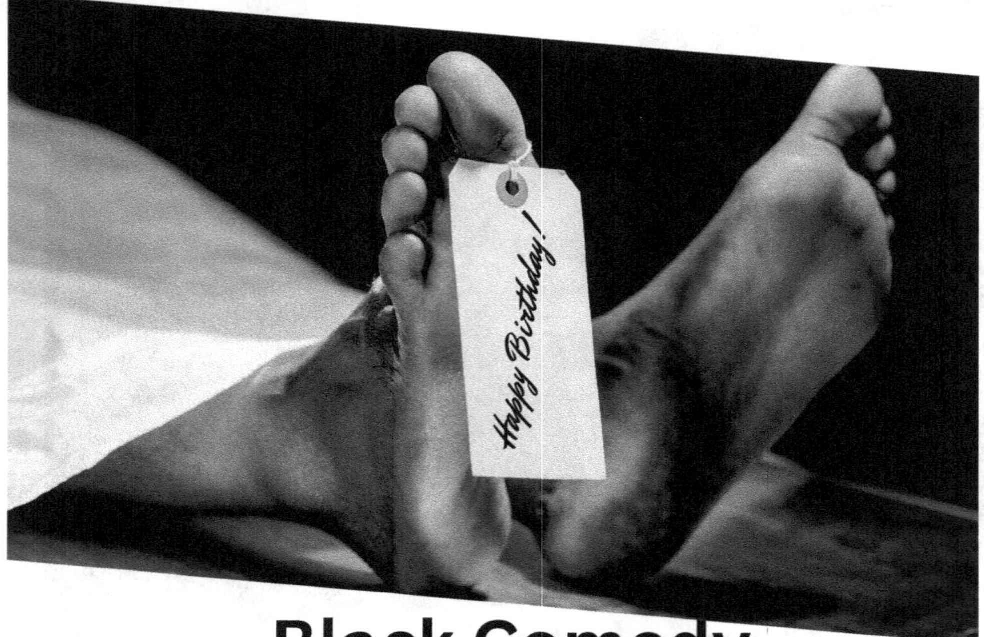

Black Comedy

Play it Straight	Morbid humor stemming from something you feel you really shouldn't laugh at, but do, often at the rather fatal expense of other people.
Downplayed	Humor that isn't necessarily grim as much as it's slapstick comedy, harm is still done to the characters, but it's not severe enough to cause death.
Exaggerated	Humor that outright crosses the line, something that should be horrible, but ends up prompting laughter anyways.
Subverted	A character tells a dark joke, and it doesn't go over well with the audience, often prompting thrown tomatoes.
Zig-Zag	A character tells a dark joke, and it goes over poorly, prompting the joker to be whacked in the head with a bat, which prompts the audience to laugh.
Deconstructed	The jokes end up losing that funny/entertaining element to them and people begin to ignore them/stop using them, in favor of more light-hearted jokes/comedy.
Reconstructed	...But people begin to miss the dark humor after a while, and those jokes begin to inch their way back into a character's joke book.
Averted	There is no humor in the setting. Whether this is due to the story being dead-serious or simply a matter of no one prompting a joke, there's no black comedy to be had.
Lampshading	"You know, I really shouldn't have laughed at that tag. I feel horrible now."
Invoked	A character tells a dark joke during a tense moment to try and lighten the mood, how well this goes depends on whether it's played straight or subverted.

The Stoic

Play it Straight A character who maintains an indifferent, impervious looking perspective on the world and their life, oftentimes appearing rather deadpan as a result. Despite this, they still carry emotions.

Downplayed The character is stoic, but they can laugh alongside others via jokes, or be deeply saddened by a loss like anyone else.

Exaggerated The character is literally unflinching before everything. No harm, words or ideas will stop them from doing as they please, almost becoming an implacable man in the process.

Subverted The character appears to be a stoic, only to be dissociating or anxious the whole time, which may *lead* into stoicism, but isn't stoicism itself.

Zig-Zag The character appears to be a stoic, indifferent and unbothered by life's events, but they were actually "out of body," and couldn't exactly respond normally, but due to that, they eventually adopt a stoic demeanor.

Deconstructed The stoic eventually begins to crack and wonder if their philosophical "brute force" is really worth it, as they feel directly responsible for some mistakes, and begin to have a mental breakdown.

Reconstructed ...But after all of that, they power through, understanding that they couldn't have caused *everything* to go poorly, and may adapt their philosophy for some leniency in the process.

Averted Every character shows emotions, and are fine with people being emotional and hurt, not wanting to take the humanity out of themselves or others.

Lampshading "So uh, do you ever smile?..."

Invoked Due to other peoples' morale going down the drain, someone decides to adopt the philosophy, not letting events, actions and words harm them as a means to keep everyone's morales up.

The Determinator

Play it Straight	The determinator is a character who pushes through extreme odds to ensure that their goal is met, whether for their own good or for someone else's sake.
Downplayed	A character has immense willpower, often attempting to uphold their own vow to themself or someone else, but they may deviate from it at some point, before going back on track.
Exaggerated	Literally nothing will keep this character down. Being shot, stabbed, blown up and outright failing their objective will mean very little, and they're still try to succeed at their goal anyway.
Subverted	A character carries immense willpower, but ends up suffering a life altering wound that completely changes their perceptions, prompting them to give up.
Zig-Zag	A character has immense willpower and determination, refusing to stay down until they lose an arm. They lose hope afterwards, until they're snapped out of it and go back to their goal despite the handicap.
Deconstructed	The determination and refusal to give up causes the character to make stupid or impossible decisions, often to the detriment of themself and their allies/friends.
Reconstructed	...Though they end up making their hazardous decisions work regardless, out of sheer willpower and prowess combined.
Averted	Everyone has limits to what they want to do, or can physically do, and as such know that it's sometimes better to give up.
Lampshading	"Seriously, does *anything* keep you down? I feel like you'd walk off a bullet to the head!"
Invoked	A character is told that they give up too easily, and to show immense determination to reach their goals. The character takes this to an extreme and flat-out *never* gives up, whether for better or worse.

Ax Crazy

Play it Straight The character is completely insane, often to a violent degree. Many different ax crazy characters should have different reasons for their madness and *especially* violence, so be careful with writing these.

Downplayed A character shows violent tendencies out of the blue, but it's either played for laughs, or simply an off-and-on occurrence that doesn't cause much harm, if at all.

Exaggerated The character is constantly foaming at the mouth with an unusually large arsenal of weapons to hunt people down with. Again, be mindful with mental illness when writing such a character.

Subverted A character appears to be completely insane, carrying large knives around and smirking here and there, but they're ultimately harmless, or end up helping people using said knives.

Zig-Zag A completely crazed maniac ends up being a nice person, but that's simply a front in order to claim more lives without suspicion.

Deconstructed The character ends up giving off too many warning signs, whether by people around them disappearing or them appearing battered, and people begin to point fingers at the maniac.

Reconstructed ...But despite this, they have a concrete alibi, and manage to toss suspicion off onto someone else, leaving them to escape and find easier victims to go after.

Averted The setting doesn't have any characters who are insane, *or* any truly violent characters. As such, the combination of insane + violent and capable, are not possible within the story.

Lampshading "So uh, does he always carrying a chainsaw and stash saws within his coat or something?..."

Invoked A character ends up being driven insane by another as an experiment, and wants to retaliate against them for inflicting this madness upon them.

The Hero Dies

Play it Straight	The protagonist or central focus character dies, and if done at the end of the story, often leads to a side character's perspective narrating what happened afterwards.
Downplayed	The hero ends up suffering a fatal blow, but ends up recovering, albeit in a much more limited state. This can be used to make future fights more tense with the weakened hero, or they can be a mentor figure.
Exaggerated	The hero is flat-out eviscerated, before being blown into ashes and having their ashes launched into the sun. Bonus points if this is done with little development to lead into the actual protagonist.
Subverted	The hero is blown up, but at the last minute they save their allies from the villain's grasp, having survived the explosion all along.
Zig-Zag	...But once the hero lands the finishing blow on the villain, they eventually succumb to the wounds from the explosion, and rest with their main objective finished.
Deconstructed	The hero dies to an established disease or inevitable conclusion, and there isn't much fanfare going around when they die.
Reconstructed	...So their friends make sure to cherish them, making sure their efforts weren't for nothing and finishing what the hero started.
Averted	The villain fires a weapon of mass destruction that hits the hero, seemingly blowing them up, only for them to walk out of the debris immediately after.
Lampshading	"Well, nothing's gonna be the same without them..."
Invoked	The hero willingly sacrifices themself to take down the villain, placing faith in their allies to ensure that their actions aren't squandered.

Curb-Stomp Battle

Play it Straight	Two characters fight, and the odds are entirely in one side's favor. There's hardly much of a "fight" as much as it's one character trying to survive the other's wrath/prowess/luck/'etc.
Downplayed	Two characters fight, and one wins against the other with very little issue, although they did sustain some damage in the process.
Exaggerated	The main antagonist "fights" someone whose legs are rendered useless. Literal curb stomping may ensue, but it's barely even a fight.
Subverted	A character fights another with hardly any issue, battering them down, only for the receiving party to simply get up and immediately fight back on equal footing.
Zig-Zag	...Which prompts the antagonist to begin trying as well, immediately throwing the fight back in their favor as a result.
Deconstructed	The result of the curb stomp battle prompts the character's allies to chew them out on it, potentially changing their opinion on the winner as a result.
Reconstructed	...But they realize that it was necessary, fighting as dirty and quickly as possible against someone who could instantly kill you is the safest way to go about fighting them.
Averted	A character established to be terrifyingly powerful goes up against a seemingly normal person, and ends up drawing out the fight or immediately losing.
Lampshading	"4 seconds is all that fight took? Did you give them a chance?"
Invoked	The enemy has the ability to immediately kill somebody on touch, or seeing them, so the protagonist fires countless bullets into them before they have a chance to activate their power.

11th-Hour Superpower

Play it Straight A character at death's door near the end of the story manages to awaken or upgrade their existing superpower or abilities, allowing them to take back victory before it's too late in glorious fashion.

Downplayed The protagonist, beaten by the antagonist, proceeds to get back up with their willpower and realize the full potential of their existing abilities.

Exaggerated The protagonist awakens a story-breaker power at the last 85-90% of the story, and proceeds to issue an unrivaled curb stomp against the antagonist and their forces.

Subverted The protagonist is on their last leg, seemingly about to go back into the fight when one of their best friends and/or crew awakens a new power, rushing in to save them with it.

Zig-Zag ...Which gets them swatted down, prompting the protagonist proper to awaken *theirs* to save their best friend.

Deconstructed The character's newfound power ends up making life too easy for them, and they proceed to slack off, put the least effort into matters and may even grow corrupt as a result.

Reconstructed ...Only for a substantial threat to emerge, prompting them to utilize their power in a much more serious manner.

Averted The protagonist is beaten down by the antagonist, they look as if they're about to gain a new power, only to simply get back up and stumble back into the fight with a second wind.

Lampshading "Well, since you've gotten that shiny new superpower, I guess I'm not needed here anymore."

Invoked The mentor intentionally leads the hero into a high risk situation, expecting them to awaken their hidden powers and reach their full potential, how successful this is depends on the setting.

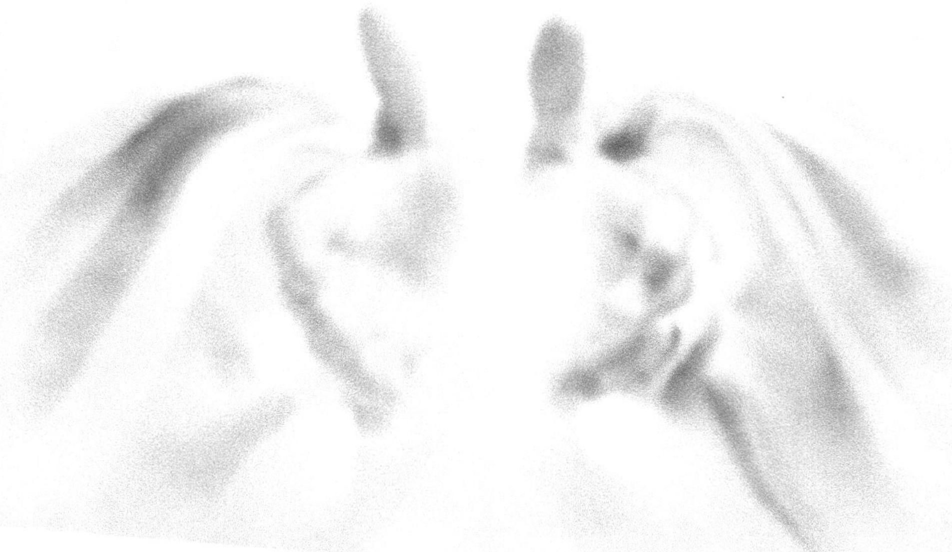

Story-Breaker Superpower

Play it Straight	The protagonist or antagonist either starts off with or obtains a superpower that makes every single threat in the story laughable by comparison.
Downplayed	The protagonist or antagonist have a power that makes short work of most threats they go up against, but relies on certain circumstances or conditions to function.
Exaggerated	The superpower quite literally breaks the story apart, whether making every single threat nonexistent (and therefor the central conflict,) or *literally* breaking the story itself.
Subverted	A superpower has immense power, but ends up coming with requirements that no one would feasibly achieve in order to use it.
Zig-Zag	...Which while it *is* useless for the majority of the story, its criteria is eventually met, causing it to become an 11th-hour superpower for the protagonist to sweep victory out from under the antagonist.
Deconstructed	The character with the power in question is thrown into every single problem without a concern for their wellbeing, causing them to be treated more as a weapon than a person.
Reconstructed	...But someone eventually comes along to treat them as a valid person, and a (sub)plot to help them realize that is set into motion as a result.
Averted	A character says that they have the ability to stop time, meaning they could theoretically do anything within that stopped time, but they actually stop time for 2 seconds. Strong, but not story-breaking.
Lampshading	*"How is that even **remotely** fair?!"*
Invoked	Knowing that the risk of failure outweighs the risk of the protagonist having this power, a divine figure imbues the protagonist with such godly capabilities that they stomp the villain in mere seconds.

Everyman

Play it Straight A completely average person with normal hobbies, work and priorities. Not restricted to male characters by any means, and they tend to be decent at a variety of things.

Downplayed A character is mostly average, with some things setting them apart from the rest, whether it be interests or their appearance.

Exaggerated They have the most typical interests you could imagine, look generic enough that no one can remember what they look like *and* their name is John/Jane Doe.

Subverted A character has a generic name and seems pretty typical, but one wardrobe change later, they're someone who stands out in a crowd.

Zig-Zag ...Except for the fact that they're in an area where dressing in flamboyant and out-there manners are commonplace, making them stand in even more.

Deconstructed The everyman gets tired of being or appearing so normal, and tries to stand out until they're noticed, pushing some boundaries in the process.

Reconstructed ...Though they eventually realize that fitting in isn't that bad, and it's not worth causing trouble to change that. Depending on the setting, this could be seen as a "victory" or "defeat" to the audience.

Averted A character has average interests, a typical name and looks normal, but they end up being fleshed out as a unique character and have some unique traits that they kept hidden.

Lampshading "Wow, you'd blend into a crowd better than trained spies by being yourself!"

Invoked A character decides to forge a false identity who is average on every scale to avoid being tracked down or to aid in infiltration.

Fish out of Water

Play it Straight	A character is tossed into an entirely different setting than they came from. This is a super trope to Fish out of Temporal Water and Trapped in Another World.
Downplayed	A character is kidnapped and awakens in an entirely different nation, having to learn their culture and language(s) to survive.
Exaggerated	The character blinks, and is in an entirely different universe altogether with no other explanation as to how they got there.
Subverted	A character seemingly wakes up in a different universe, with unfamiliar languages and formalities, only for them to realize that they're in a different nation.
Zig-Zag	...But this nation is completely different from their world's version of it, and they realize that they really *did* travel into a different universe.
Deconstructed	The character, having been thrown into a vastly different place/time can't figure out the language(s) or culture, and ends up being detained, or *worse.*
Reconstructed	...But they're busted out by someone who speaks their language, and they're quickly mentored on the way of life for this new world.
Averted	The protagonist goes to sleep, expecting to wake up in a different land with the wonders that ensue, only to wake up in their same old bed.
Lampshading	"You, uh... don't look like you're from around here."
Invoked	A character's world or galaxy is dying, so they attempt to find a means to escape it, whether by magic, technology or some other means.

Fish out of Temporal Water

Play it Straight	Something happens to a character, prompting them to either awaken in, or travel to a different time period.
Downplayed	A character gets sent a few decades into the past, not much learning is necessary, but they still have some things to get used to.
Exaggerated	A character is catapulted millions of years back, and has to adapt to the prehistoric ecosystem around them.
Subverted	A character awakens, being told that they were asleep for 2 years. Not much has changed since then, and the character has very little to catch up with.
Zig-Zag	...Except for the impending war that's been brewing the last year, which catches them by surprise and no one else.
Deconstructed	The character being tossed into a different time may result in their untimely demise, whether by barbaric medieval raiders or prosecution in a futuristic setting.
Reconstructed	...But they learn quickly, and end up adapting to the time they've been thrown into, growing them as a person in the process.
Averted	A character awakens, being told that they've been asleep for 2 years. They gasp in horror, only to be told that it was a joke.
Lampshading	"Look who walked out of a museum."
Invoked	A character has to travel back in time to save the present/future, so they brush up on their history to figure out the best plan of attack.

Trapped in Another World

Play it Straight A character is sent to, or awakens in a different world. They attempt to figure out the workings of the world, find people to guide them the right way and try to find their place in this new frontier.

Downplayed A character is thrown into a secret society, having to live a double life while learning the workings of this newfound "world" around them.

Exaggerated The character is thrown into an entirely different dimension with totally different concepts and science. Good luck surviving such an environment.

Subverted A character walks through a portal, only for it to be an elaborate setup with a hole in the wall leading to a falsified "world."

Zig-Zag ...Until an actual portal forms itself, causing the characters to fall into a different world in the middle of their gag/show/etc.

Deconstructed The setting proves too dangerous for the character, and they're quickly trampled over by the wildlife, or executed by the dominant life forms.

Reconstructed ...But they're given an 11th-hour superpower before their execution, giving them the necessary boost to survive this harsh new world.

Averted A character walks through a portal in their wall, only for their friends to reveal that it was a staged act, and that they're on the same planet.

Lampshading "Well, wer sure aren't in Kansas anymore."

Invoked Due to resource shortages, a government decides to send a select few to other universes or planets in hopes to gather crucial materials and resources.

Yes, seriously...

Running Gag

Play it Straight	A character is constantly kicking doors down instead of opening them, prompting them to enter most scenes destroying public or private property.
Downplayed	A character has the same comedic event happen to/via them on two or three separate occasions and in a much less drastic manner.
Exaggerated	The character's running gag happens every single scene that they're in, and ends up altering the story in magnitude every time it does.
Subverted	A character has a recurring joke, until someone ends up shooting it down or gets hurt by it, prompting the character to drop it.
Zig-Zag	...But they go right back to it later on, whether due to being away from the complainer, or simply not caring what the consequences are.
Deconstructed	The repeated gags end up causing serious problems, doors being broken down rack up costs and end up getting the character arrested.
Reconstructed	...Until they break the cell door open the very next scene, promptly escaping prison *through* their running gag.
Averted	A character makes a joke/does something amusing, and does it again, only to drop it without much explanation afterwards.
Lampshading	"Okay, just how many fines has your crusade against doors racked up now?!"
Invoked	A character decides to have a running gag as an identifying trait, so their allies know where they've been through the trail of broken doors.

Brick Joke

Play it Straight A character throws a brick into the sky. Two scenes later, it lands nearby or on a character, knocking them unconscious.

Downplayed A character throws a brick into the sky. Within the same scene, it lands on someone to emphasize a character's point, with comedic effect.

Exaggerated A character throws a bowling ball *really* high up at the start of the story. Near the end, when the villain has the protagonist on their last leg, the bowling ball hits the villain and renders them unconscious.

Subverted A character throws their cellphone up into the sky, the phone lands elsewhere and the thrower recovers it afterwards.

Zig-Zag ...Though it was someone else's phone, and as they return the stranger's phone to them, the thrower's phone hits the stranger in the face, knocking them unconscious and cracking the screen.

Deconstructed The thrower goes about their journey, only for the brick to land and hit someone in the face, putting them in a coma that causes the brick thrower to feel guilty.

Reconstructed ...Until it's revealed that the comatose recipient was actually the main villain, and they were about to kill off one of the main characters.

Averted A character throws a toilet paper roll into the sky, and throughout the story, it never lands or is mentioned again.

Lampshading "So, we're go- OW! Where did that brick even come from?!"

Invoked A character has insanely good luck that twists every odd to their favor, so as insurance, they throw a brick extremely high up to land on a potential threat's head.

Heroic Sacrifice

Play it Straight	A character tackles the protagonist out of the way, but ends up getting shot in the process. They say their parting words with the protagonist before dying.
Downplayed	A character dives in front of the protagonist and is shot as a result, though the bullet had grazed them, they're taken out of action until they get better.
Exaggerated	A character lunges toward the protagonist, knocking them out of the way of an anti-material beam. They're immediately evaporated for their efforts and are hailed as more of a hero than the protagonist.
Subverted	A character dives in front of a gunshot to save the protagonist, but once they both get up, they look at themselves and realize that the protagonist was hit instead.
Zig-Zag	...With the protagonist being grazed by the bullet, and the savior shot clean through. The savior proceeds to collapse, and dies shortly after.
Deconstructed	The savior dying to ensure the protagonist's survival means that the group's strongest fighter is now dead, and the remaining heroes are completely outmatched as a result.
Reconstructed	...But not wanting to let their sacrifice be in vain, the protagonist and/or their allies push through, awakening new abilities to slaughter their enemies for taking their ally from them.
Averted	The would-be savior tackles the protagonist out of a bullet's path, and they check themselves for any wounds, both remain perfectly intact and they continue the fight.
Lampshading	"You know, you really were too good for your own good..."
Invoked	The mentor decides that their time is up, and the hero has a much better chance at stopping the overarching threat, so they make peace with the inevitable outcome and save the hero.

Foreshadowing

Play it Straight	The hero's love interest mentions that she got bitten by a mosquito. Later in the story, she falls ill and the hero tries to find a cure for her.
Downplayed	The hero's love interest mentions that she got bitten by a mosquito. Later, she feels a little ill, but nothing bad enough to warrant any concerns.
Exaggerated	The hero's love interest is bitten by a mosquito, their mother is sneezed on by a sick person and their group boards a plane with a coughing passenger. The hero is completely alone on the final battle.
Subverted	The hero's love interest mentions that she got bitten by a mosquito. Nothing arises of it, and they both take on the villain's forces.
Zig-Zag	...Until she feels ill midway, which progressively gets worse until they're just about to fight the villain. The hero has to handle the fight on his own, and quickly in order to help her afterwards.
Deconstructed	The love interest ends up feeling like she's let the hero down, or vice versa, and tensions begin to boil between the two as a result.
Reconstructed	...But the two realize how stupid it is to argue over something that neither side had a hand in causing, and move on from the ordeal.
Averted	The hero's love interest mentions that she got bitten by a mosquito. Ultimately, nothing ever comes of it, and they both fight the villain together.
Lampshading	"I sure hope this bite doesn't result in me falling horribly ill or anything."
Invoked	The love interest knows that she will likely fall ill, but she can't find the will to outright say it, so she simply mentions the bite and hopes that the hero will catch on.

Exactly What It Says on the Tin

Play it Straight Someone mentions a blue dog. When the protagonist is shown the "blue dog," it is indeed a dog that happens to be dyed blue.

Downplayed Someone mentions a blue dog. When the protagonist is shown the "blue dog," it's actually named "blue dog," and isn't actually blue.

Exaggerated Someone mentions a humongous fire-breathing blue dog with the personality of a saint. When the protagonist sees the aforementioned dog, everything lines up perfectly with the description.

Subverted Someone mentions a humongous fire-breathing blue dog with the personality of a saint. When the protagonist sees the aforementioned dog, it *is* blue and nice, but nothing else lines up.

Zig-Zag ...Until it sneezes, which causes it to expand into a massive dog while accidentally burning the place down in the process.

Deconstructed Mentioning the dog in such detail leads the characters into believing that it's *exactly* as described, so when they go to search for it, they can't find it because it notably lacks one of the eye-catching qualities.

Reconstructed ...Until they realize that they missed a spot, and it's right there in front of them, exactly as it they had been expecting.

Averted Someone mentions a blue dog. When the protagonist looks for a blue dog, they find dogs and cats, but none that happen to be *blue.*

Lampshading "What does this vehicle *mean* by it being fueled with banana- oh."

Invoked A company or government wants to ensure that citizens are safe when treading hazardous areas, so they list the hazards with a bright sign at the entrance. Odds are that some people ignore it anyway.

Character Development

Play it Straight A character is portrayed as a trembling coward, and throughout the story, they learn how to overcome their fears and move on from them.

Downplayed The character is portrayed as a trembling coward, and throughout the story, they progress further and further through their fears, but still have some ways to go at the story's resolution.

Exaggerated A character is portrayed as a constantly terrified coward who can't speak a single word. One scene later, they're absolutely fearless and carry immense charisma.

Subverted A character decides to stop drinking, but during a mental breakdown proceeds to fall back into alcoholism.

Zig-Zag ...But of their own free will or others' advice, they make this drink the last, and make an attempt to go clean, for good.

Deconstructed A character develops throughout the story, but with the beneficial habits and changes come more detrimental ones. A former coward may become reckless.

Reconstructed ...But people don't stop developing, and this reckless behavior and trauma can eventually be put to rest, techniques can be used to calm down and the character can do their best to move on.

Averted A character discusses their fears of the deep sea before a boating trip, and while their friends convince them to try and work past it, they ultimately don't by the end of the story.

Lampshading "Wow, you sure couldn't have made that leap a week ago."

Invoked Tired of their friend's immense cowardice, someone plots to throw them on a journey so they can overcome their fears and grow a spine.

Large Ham

Play it Straight A character overemphasizes everything they say, tends to lack an indoor voice and blows things out of proportion on a regular basis.

Downplayed A character is usually normal, or even quiet, but when the time comes, they can blow up into a festival of ear shattering speech.

Exaggerated Every appearance this character makes is full to the brim with shouting, deafens people close by and overreacts to the slightest provocation.

Subverted A character is loud, exaggerates everything and does all that a straight large ham does, but only because they're being used as a lure for attention so their allies can sneak by.

Zig-Zag ...Until they grow to like the overly flamboyant persona, so they adopt it for most of their future missions and serve as the go-to bait.

Deconstructed A character's audacity, volume and tendency to over-exaggerate everything pushes people away due to seeing them as a loud, overly obnoxious buffoon.

Reconstructed ...But then again, there's something so strangely charismatic about the way they speak, shout and act, that people begin to go back to them because of it.

Averted A character is built up as an extremely loud, mountainous bruiser who has no indoor voice, but meeting them proper proves that claim wrong.

Lampshading "***WHAT DO YOU MEAN I'M TOO LOOOOOUUUUUUD?!*** **GET YOUR** ***EARS CHECKED, BUDDYYYYYY!***"

Invoked A character, one way or another decides that being extremely loud, confident and boisterous is going to make them more charismatic.

Suspension of Disbelief

Play it Straight A term used with books, films and games in which the audience are immersed in the work. They're more willing to believe that a character can pull a chainsaw out of a purse than they otherwise would.

Downplayed As a term for storytelling, suspension of disbelief isn't capable of being downplayed, exaggerated, zig-zagged, subverted, deconstructed or reconstructed.

Exaggerated As a term for storytelling, suspension of disbelief isn't capable of being downplayed, exaggerated, zig-zagged, subverted, deconstructed or reconstructed.

Subverted As a term for storytelling, suspension of disbelief isn't capable of being downplayed, exaggerated, zig-zagged, subverted, deconstructed or reconstructed.

Zig-Zag As a term for storytelling, suspension of disbelief isn't capable of being downplayed, exaggerated, zig-zagged, subverted, deconstructed or reconstructed.

Deconstructed To play it straight, you simply write it as it sounds. If you have a villain, the villain will do bad things and be the stereotypical villain.

Reconstructed To play it straight, you simply write it as it sounds. If you have a villain, the villain will do bad things and be the stereotypical villain.

Averted The author makes it clear that the book is unbelievable, whether with fourth-wall breaks or sheer insanity throughout.

Lampshading "Wow, that couldn't *really* happen in reality... right?"

Invoked The author wants the audience to relate and sympathize with the characters, putting them on an emotional roller-coaster throughout to keep them hooked on the book.

Rule of Cool

Play it Straight	A spy dressed up in a mariachi outfit stakes out a place despite wearing an obvious outfit, proceeds to fight gunmen with a pair of maracas that don't break and walks away from an explosion without a scratch.
Downplayed	A spy dressed up in a mariachi outfit stakes out a place by blending in with a band, uses his maracas to knock someone out for their weapon and survives a blast while sustaining some injury.
Exaggerated	Every single character is doing back flips, kung-fu gunfights and wears extremely impractical outfits without any drawback.
Subverted	A spy dressed up in a mariachi outfit stakes out a place despite wearing an obvious outfit, but they're eventually caught and shot at as a result.
Zig-Zag	A spy dressed up in a mariachi outfit infiltrates a crime syndicate's meeting, but is found and has to ditch his disguise, but he manages to slam the maracas he brought into the criminals' faces afterwards.
Deconstructed	The spy works for a government branch that strictly adheres to professionalism and by-the-books methods, so the spy ends up fired, or targeted by an assassin shortly after.
Reconstructed	...Only for the spy to tackle their would-be assassin out of their penthouse window, having a fistfight as they fall and landing with some scrapes and bruises, while the assassin lands on a car.
Averted	A character sees a poster of a soldier choking an alien with one hand as he stomps another down. Inspired by the feats of awesomeness, they sign up and shortly realize that it's nowhere near as glorious.
Lampshading	"It honestly feels like you *need* to do things as awesomely as you can fathom to sustain yourself."
Invoked	A character, whether due to their powers or the setting, literally *needs* to do things in extremely flashy and cool ways to gain more power, lower their enemies' morale or keep themselves alive.

Catchphrase

Play it Straight A character is known for saying "cut me some slack," and will say that quite frequently when prompted with a tedious task.

Downplayed A character says "cut me some slack," when prompted to do over a dozen things, but says so in different variations.

Exaggerated A character pretty much punctuates every sentence with their catchphrase, oftentimes annoying everyone around them as a result.

Subverted After being given a list of things to do, the character begins to say "cut me some slack," only to be cut-off mid-sentence by another character.

Zig-Zag ...And shortly after the others leave for their own responsibilities, the character says their catchphrase to themself.

Deconstructed The group is sneaking behind enemy lines, disguised as troops. One of the characters says their catchphrase mid-conversation, which ends up alerting their enemies who's familiar with it.

Reconstructed ...But they just so happen to have a really popular catchphrase, and the enemies believe that it's borrowed from somebody else. They converse about it afterwards.

Averted When told to do something, the character says "cut me some slack," but the next time they're told to do something later, they reply with "ugh, really?..."

Lampshading "Really, it's just getting some groceries. You don't need to say that every single time you're asked to do something, you know."

Invoked The character, tired of being saddled with loads and loads of work, decides to make a catchphrase to annoy everyone who puts more stuff on their to-do list.

Action Girl

Play it Straight	A female character who carries her own weight, often jumping into the front lines to save the day alongside her more combat-oriented allies.
Downplayed	A female character who is capable of filling in a more action-oriented role if no one else is on hand. Her effectiveness isn't as good as the original hero, but she can still fight better than any other option.
Exaggerated	A female character who stomps entire armies alone, lives for the thrill of the fight and beats every single guy in arm-wrestling despite her size.
Subverted	She beats up bad guys, saves the day and knows how to handle herself, but she does so because she's outright forced to, when she'd rather be on the sidelines.
Zig-Zag	...But she eventually grows to enjoy it, and feels a sense of lack when the action's died down. Once things begin again, she dives right in.
Deconstructed	Due to her taking the reins, she earns the ire of her allies, sustains damage that eventually begins to add up and she *really* starts to feel lost without a fight going on, which may prompt more risks.
Reconstructed	...But her allies warm up to her for her help, and support her when she feels down due to feeling that "uselessness" that comes after a large-scale conflict.
Averted	She tries to put up a fight against the villain, but all of her attempts to fight them ends in failure. After a short while, she throws in the towel and decides to provide support in other forms.
Lampshading	"Sheesh, I feel like you're better at breaking their bones than half the *guys* on your side."
Invoked	Due to running out of soldiers, a military decides to use propaganda, abduction or more friendlier means to recruit and train women to act as re-enforcements.

The Reveal

Play it Straight The villain is defeated, the protagonist walks to their defeated foe to unmask them, and sees that the villain was really their long lost brother all along!

Downplayed The villain is defeated, the protagonist walks to their defeated foe and unmasks them to confirm their suspicions on who it was, and they're right!

Exaggerated The villain is defeated, the protagonist walks up to their defeated foe and wakes up, realizing that their entire adventure was a dream.

Subverted The villain is defeated and at death's door. He tells the protagonist that he's actually their long lost brother... but it's a complete lie since the protagonist is an only-child.

Zig-Zag ...Because the villain was erased from history, and his family hid him from the world in order to prevent harm/panic/etc.

Deconstructed Due to the protagonist not remembering that the villain was really their brother this whole time, they can't be bothered with seeing them die, and the reveal falls short.

Reconstructed ...Until later, when they think back to that moment and feel guilty about letting their brother die, since they could've changed things.

Averted The villain wears no mask, and the protagonist immediately recognizes them on TV from early on, prompting no real surprise.

Lampshading "Wow, I was *not* expecting that face behind the mask."

Invoked The villain wears a mask during all of their campaigns to keep themself anonymous, and to surprise the protagonist with a reveal for an opportunity to stab/shoot them.

Pet the Dog

Play it Straight The villain, amidst him shooting his own henchmen for fun, taking hostages for money and other cruel acts, pets a cat on the side of a street and leaves a bowl of food for it.

Downplayed The villain, amidst him shooting his own henchmen for kicks, taking hostages for money, and other cruel acts, pets a cat on the side of a street.

Exaggerated The villain, amidst him shooting his own henchmen for whatever other reason a villain has to do such a thing, takes a cat and her litter of kittens to a vet, and adopts them shortly after to take care of.

Subverted The villain pets a cat on the side of a road because he's being monitored, and wants to appear as a moral person to retain his cover.

Zig-Zag ...But another day, he encounters the cat again, and decides to pet it and give it a bowl of food out of sincerity.

Deconstructed The villain attempted to pet the cat to improve his public image while live on-air, but it does absolutely nothing to help everyone's perception of him despite his one good deed.

Reconstructed ...But he was charmed by the cat's purring, and *negotiates*, in his own way, to adopt the cat for himself to pet on-demand.

Averted The villain is handed a cat to pet by an advisor to help increase his image, but he tosses the cat aside and demands to handle it his way.

Lampshading "Wow, maybe his heart isn't completely black. Just *mostly*."

Invoked After advising him time and time again, the villain eventually caves in and adopts one of the advisor's cats after his house was destroyed. The villain warms up to the fluff ball shortly after.

Only Sane Man

Play it Straight A character keeps their low-key insane allies in check, the plans are run by her to ensure that things don't go out of hand and she's often the real leader amongst the crew.

Downplayed Their allies have some quirks here and there, but this girl's the best bet for the most logical plans and she knows how to handle his crew better than any other leader.

Exaggerated The entire world is full to the brim of insane people who solve things impractically, this character uses common sense and outperforms the outrageous opponents with logic.

Subverted Her allies are all outlandish and unorthodox, so this character appears to be the sane one by comparison, only to take everything in a mechanical manner with the mannerisms of a machine.

Zig-Zag ...But despite being bound to logic and nearly emotionless, she is still the most functional member of her crew, and decent enough to get along with as well.

Deconstructed The numerous hijinks of the characters surrounding her causes immense stress, strain and, at times, outright harm to her, causing her to consider quitting.

Reconstructed ...But she realizes that the crew can't survive without her, and she's grown attached to them as well. Getting a hold of herself, she ensures that she'll manage her stress and stay out of harm's way.

Averted She seems calm, sensible and affable until the drawing board comes out, revealing a massive machine of destruction to defeat one person with.

Lampshading "So uh, you their babysitter?"

Invoked This character was just as impractical as the rest, but decided that she needed to be more practical to offset the group's madness.

Too Dumb to Live

Play it Straight	This character opts to run into the wilderness of death with absolutely nothing for self-defense, and promptly dies.
Downplayed	He brings a knife and lighter, but still runs into the wilderness of death with little else and is maimed as a result.
Exaggerated	He's met with two doors, one reading "live," the other "die." He opens the door labeled "die" and is blasted by a shotgun rigged to the door.
Subverted	He packed no weapons, and goes to fight the big bad. He surprises the big bad when he ends up fighting using his belt to a standstill despite being underprepared.
Zig-Zag	...Which did little more than make for an entertaining fight, and he still dies afterwards due to the big bad using real weapons.
Deconstructed	His stupid decision ends up having his allies restrain him and hold him captive so he can't do any other stupid acts.
Reconstructed	...But then he starts playing with the various chemicals in his crew's base, and proceeds to blow himself up with an acidic-explosion-radioactive-etc reaction.
Averted	Having heard that the big bad killed his family, he runs out to fight him only to stop himself when he realizes that he's not prepared for a fight.
Lampshading	"Excuse me, *how have you made it this far?*"
Invoked	He's acting intentionally stupid and "dies" in order to break off from the group and find something else to do.

The Load

Play it Straight This character simply follows along, accompanies the crew for something new and... does little else, often needing to be saved by his crew.

Downplayed He's capable of putting up a good fight and supporting the crew, but his bad luck or limitations ends up putting him in lots of danger.

Exaggerated He's a leech that surfs couches, eats up the crew's entire stash of food and ends up kidnapped by the big bad more than any princess, prized pet or politician.

Subverted He's the weakest link of the group so the big bad can kidnap him for ransom. The moment he's in the enemy's captivity, he breaks out and rampages their armies from within.

Zig-Zag ...In his mind, and in reality, he's really a useless load who got kidnapped as ransom that no one really wants to trade for.

Deconstructed Due to him doing no good for the crew, they slowly distance away from him and switch hideouts without telling him, refusing to bring him back in.

Reconstructed ...And somehow despite that, he finds his way back to them, hops on their couch and eats all of their potato chips until he's kidnapped *again.*

Averted His resume says that he's hardly held any real jobs, but he assures that this line of work is ideal for him, and that it is.

Lampshading "Uh, what's that guy over there good for again?"

Invoked Every crew needs a weak link to draw the enemy's attention, so a pragmatic and unsavory crew will employ an everyman to act as the bait of the bunch.

Noodle Incident

Play it Straight	A past event that the crew dares not speak about. Any mention of it is met with hushes and faces going pale.
Downplayed	A past event that the crew is wary of. Any mention of it will be met with some looks, before people continue doing what they were beforehand.
Exaggerated	Mentioning the past event causes the crew to immediately point all of their weapons at the questioner, while sweating in terror. They come to agree on changing the subject,
Subverted	A character mentions the past event, and everyone grows silent, looking on, before eventually laughing it off as one crewmate explains the incident.
Zig-Zag	...Which was a fabrication, and the real event is still left completely unspoken and kept safeguarded so no one really knows what happened.
Deconstructed	Something crucial ended up happening during the incident, and the characters left out on it need to know what happened to deal with current matters.
Reconstructed	...The elements that help the crew with the pressing issue is said, and that's out of the way, but the remaining horrors of the incident remain unspoken.
Averted	A horribly embarrassing incident involving the worst of the crew's cooks trying to make a buffet for everyone is revealed in full detail, though no one likes to be reminded of it regardless.
Lampshading	"Wow, I wish I had a time machine so I could see what actually happened there."
Invoked	The original crewmates decide to make a fake incident that no one speaks of in order to mess with newbies and their curiosity.

Even Evil has Standards

Play it Straight The villain has an evil empire, plunders resources and performs all sorts of villainy, but the line is drawn when his general attempts genocide, promptly dealing with the general himself.

Downplayed The villain has an evil empire, plunders resources and performs all sorts of villainy, but when his general proposes genocide, he's quick to shut it down and move on.

Exaggerated The villain has a satellite laser to nuke everyone who he believes to be worse than himself off the face of the planet, and uses it frequently.

Subverted The villain detests his general's plan on-stage, but behind the curtain, they agree to it as long as it's under wraps.

Zig-Zag ...But he said that just to get the general to be quiet about it, and really isn't along for the ride, instead planning on making it fail.

Deconstructed The villain attempting to get rid of his general ends up prompting a fight from the general and his men, who all outnumber the villain drastically.

Reconstructed ...But they're all reminded just *how* the villain got to where he is now, as he promptly eviscerates the general's forces and slaughters the general by himself.

Averted In a boardroom meeting, the villain and his advisors are discussing plans when his general mentions genocide. His advisors plead against it, but he agrees.

Lampshading "Just how bad was that guy if *you* thought he was in the wrong?!"

Invoked As a test for the villain, the hero disguises as an advisor and proposes a plan so deeply disturbing and vile, that he'd *have* to disagree with it, in order to find out whether he's worth redeeming.

Nice Job Breaking It, Hero

Play it Straight The hero beats the villain, and visits him in a special holding cell. Without noticing, she accidentally gives him a way out before she leaves, prompting the villain to escape shortly after.

Downplayed The hero beats the villain, and visits him in a special holding cell. Shortly after leaving the holding cell, the hero realizes that she left the door open, and runs back into the villain, having broken out.

Exaggerated The hero beats the villain, and visits him in a special holding cell. Without noticing, she had accidentally unlocked every single cell in the prison. unleashing every supervillain held there.

Subverted The hero beats the villain, and visits him in a special holding cell. While she ends up leaving the door open, she remembers before the villain can escape.

Zig-Zag ...Patting herself on the back, the hero leaves the prison, completely oblivious to the fact that she left the door unlocked.

Deconstructed The hero ends up feeling immensely guilty for letting the villain go free again, and her allies are scolding her for being so clumsy.

Reconstructed ...But she decides that she won't give up, and *will* find the villain again, with the intent to keep him behind bars for good.

Averted The hero checks pays attention to what she should do during the visit, follows the orders to a tee and almost forgets to lock the door, but does so as the villain stomps his feet in the background.

Lampshading "How could you *possibly* leave that door unlocked? Were you trying to break him out?!"

Invoked The hero feels underwhelmed with how she stopped the villain, and intentionally leaves an exit for him so they can clash again on better terms.

Chekhov's Gun

Play it Straight A repeater rifle hangs over the entry of a saloon. Later in the series, when the crew returns to the saloon, they're attacked and grab the rifle to fight with.

Downplayed A bell sits on the bar of a saloon. Later that scene, when assailants hold people hostage inside, one of the crewmates grabs the bell and throws it at one of the assailants.

Exaggerated In the very first chapter, a repeater rifle hangs over the entry of a saloon. In the final chapter of the series, they return to the saloon and use the rifle to resolve the plot.

Subverted A rifle sits behind the dragon during a negotiation with one of the crew in his office. Despite the obvious weapon, the crewmate can't pick a fight here, and finishes negotiating.

Zig-Zag ...Until the dragon prompts a flat-out sadistic choice that the character will have to go through, were they to follow the dragon's orders. This breaks into a fight, and the rifle is used to wound the dragon.

Deconstructed When the crew gets a hold of the rifle, it's unloaded, and there's absolutely no ammunition nearby to load into it.

Reconstructed ...So with some tape and a knife, the crew makes an improvised spear out of it, and uses it to spear the assailants at a safer distance.

Averted A repeater rifle hangs over the entry of a saloon. When the assailants barge in and start taking hostages, the crew already has enough weaponry to handle the situation.

Lampshading "I noticed the gun on the wall earlier, had a feeling it'd serve *some* purpose if things went south. Here we are."

Invoked The leader of the crew planted some weapons in plain sight for the crew to easily obtain and use, should things go downhill.

Blood Knight

Play it Straight A fighter who thrives from combat, violence, war, all sorts of fighting. Weapons or not, he will make the battlefield into his personal playground.

Downplayed While otherwise professional, the blood knight does have fun showing off and beating his enemies up, often taking the more physical assignments when possible.

Exaggerated A herculean man of war, who instigates conflict so he can fight, conquest and ravage everyone and everything for the sake of his own enjoyment.

Subverted The fighter has a lot of fun in the midst of combat, but it's an act, as showing grief would have his allies deem them too weak.

Zig-Zag ...And after enough pretending, he eventually comes to get used to the violence, and genuinely enjoy it for all it's worth.

Deconstructed Due to their outright bloodlust, normal companies refuse to hire him, governments pay close attention to him and he's isolated due to scaring everyone.

Reconstructed ...So a PMC reaches out to him, and hires him to handle their dirty work with the promise of glory and action.

Averted A character is proposed as a village-burning mass-murdering barbarian, but it turns out to be propaganda, and he's not nearly as bad as portrayed.

Lampshading "Okay, you enjoy hurting people *way* too much for anyone's own good."

Invoked A corrupt general picks up someone who's desperate, and gets them used to fighting and war, proposing it as their meaning in life. When everyone's left the general, the blood knight stays because they see no other purpose in life.

Karma Houdini

Play it Straight	The villain performs horrendous acts, tortures the hero's loved ones and ends up getting away without a scratch.
Downplayed	The villain does all sorts of bad things, beats up the heroes and manages to get away, albeit with a major injury putting them out of action for a while.
Exaggerated	The villain eats kittens, burns cities and throws heroes into fates worse than death. Not only do they get away with it easily, but they have outright *good* karma in spite of their horrible acts.
Subverted	The villain, despite all the horrible things they've done throughout the story, manages to get away, only for a character thought to be dead points a gun at their head.
Zig-Zag	...Only to laugh, telling the villain to be a bit more careful, since that could've been the end of the villain's reign.
Deconstructed	Due to the villain's numerous misdeeds, everyone starts taking extreme measures to take them down immediately if they show back up.
Reconstructed	...Which is ultimately useless, as the villain uses their enemies' paranoia against them, and laugh as they all tear each other apart.
Averted	The setting doesn't have karma, so the villain's own aptitude and influence to survive until the end of the story.
Lampshading	"Bad guys always get the best luck, don't they?"
Invoked	The heroes decide that the villain needs to survive in order to prevent the evil god within them from breaking free and causing even more destruction, buying them time to prepare.

Face-Heel Turn

Play it Straight	One of the hero's close allies ends up succumbing to their power, the influence of others or the darkness, and becomes a villain, often with an appearance makeover.
Downplayed	One of the hero's close allies begins resorting to extreme methods in order to stop their enemies, prompting shock from their allies as a result.
Exaggerated	One of the hero's allies, a pure paragon, turns into the most horrendous monster and wipes out a city when the villain insults their cooking.
Subverted	One of the hero's allies ends up betraying them and joining the villain's side, but when they're behind enemy lines, they stab the villain in the back at the cost of their own life.
Zig-Zag	...Well, that's what the news said, but the villain hijacked the network and pushed a phony story. Their ally is still on the villain's side, and is arriving back at their base without them knowing.
Deconstructed	The now-heel was too obvious with their impending switch, and the heroes end up charging them head-on.
Reconstructed	...But the villain dives in and rescues the heel, deflecting the heroes' attacks and evacuating as quickly as possible to prepare their new ally for battle.
Averted	The hero asks how the ally's powers, money and status hasn't gotten to them yet, the ally simply states that those factors mean nothing when their goal is to make the world a better place.
Lampshading	"Uh, was he underpaid or something?"
Invoked	The heroes need a mole, so they pick their best ally to "betray" them in hopes that the villain will notice and recruit them.

The Dreaded

Play it Straight The hitman, whose name being muttered in a room causes every assassin, contractor and politician to freeze in a cold sweat for a few seconds.

Downplayed The hitman, whose name is heard in a room causes every contractor to go completely silent and shudder in fear.

Exaggerated The hitman, whose name is heard on a national tv channel prompts *everyone* to widen their eyes and freeze in fear.

Subverted The hitman enters a hotel, and to their surprise, no one bats an eye, much less shudder in fear from seeing them enter.

Zig-Zag ...Until the hitman is asked of their name. Saying it causes *everyone* to freeze and look at the reception desk with looks of terror.

Deconstructed The hitman's notoriety means that surprising enemies is harder, they're isolated from everyone, often sent on impossible contracts and their enemies put the best against them.

Reconstructed ...Which means nearly nothing, as the hitman in question is just *that* good at what they do, so they use the enemy's paranoia or confidence against them in order to gain the upper hand.

Averted The hitman walks into a fancy hotel and books a room. When they're asked of their name, they give a smug expression as they say their name. The receptionist is weirded out, but nothing more happens.

Lampshading "That man, if you could even call him that, managed to kill 3 different branches of the largest mafia in the world, and *ALONE* at that!"

Invoked A politician frames their rival as a baby-eating monster through advertisements and commercials to rally more votes away from the rival.

One-Man Army

Play it Straight	The same hitman as before earned his reputation as the dreaded by fighting multiple groups of gangsters, mafioso and militaries, and winning despite the odds.
Downplayed	The hitman takes down abnormal amounts of enemies alone, but does so by utilizing the terrain, camouflage, superior equipment or simply fighting weaker opponents.
Exaggerated	The hitman is a nigh-unstoppable force of nature that has a bodycount in the thousands; in just this week alone.
Subverted	The hitman fights groups of enemies alone, but they *can* be outnumbered anywhere from 5 to 7 assailants at a time.
Zig-Zag	...So for more than 5 enemies, they begin to use the environment to their advantage for cover, distractions and weaponry to improvise with.
Deconstructed	The hitman manages to fight countless enemies off, but due to their feats, they're immensely scarred, if not actively wounded, and the odds of them having a life outside of assassination is slim to none.
Reconstructed	...But their sheer willpower gets them through it. They use extreme means to keep themself kicking as they wipe out the last of their threats before they can go home free.
Averted	Despite being built up as the dreaded, it turns out to have been a complete lie as the hitman goes down in their first fight.
Lampshading	"Well, I guess I'm going job hunting if he's going to take every assassin out of the business."
Invoked	The hitman can't get any help from outside sources, so they train relentlessly to take down multiple enemies and use their environment to win every fight as pragmatically as possible.

Mooks

Play it Straight Low-ranking fodder that the villain throws at the heroes, or just as often roaming the streets, looking for trouble to start and people to rob.

Downplayed Despite being low-ranking fodder, they're still competent enough for the hero(es) to put quite a bit of effort into fighting.

Exaggerated Mooks are throwaway thugs that the hero can stomp easily in order to show how cool they are. The only real threat is the fact that they outnumber the hero 100:1.

Subverted The hero throws a punch at one of the mooks, only for the mook to catch the punch and beat the hero up with startling ease. Expect this particular mook to return later on for a real fight.

Zig-Zag ...Until the hero blasts the mook's head off. They were simply caught off guard, and the mook wasn't anything special for beating the hero up.

Deconstructed The mooks are people too, and the hero begins to feel guilty for cutting through so many of them. Alternatively, the hero grows apathetic to killing them, turning them into a stone-cold killer.

Reconstructed ...So they opt for nonlethal means of dispatching the mooks to help with the guilt, or are forced to use nonlethal means by their allies.

Averted The hero approaches some mooks, and while 4 of them ready their weapons, another runs off in terror and doesn't want to partake in the fight.

Lampshading "Gee, their budget's gotta be real low with training and weaponry like that."

Invoked Well, the villain needs to start somewhere, so they pay the least amount of money necessary to throw goons at the hero as they prepare their elites with better equipment and training.

Mook Horror Show

Play it Straight The hero loses their mind, and starts to ravage through countless mooks, often shown from the mooks' perspective as an unstoppable monster shearing through normal-ish people.

Downplayed The hero goes berserk, and begins to rampage through a group of mooks, viciously beating them down before being calmed by an ally.

Exaggerated One person goes insane, and uses their immense power to destroy the big bad's countless armies *alone*, showing the full magnitude of their destruction.

Subverted The hero begins to slaughter mook after mook, until the villain arrives and fights them to a standstill as their mooks begin to retreat.

Zig-Zag ...But the villain actually *dies* to the furious hero, and they begin to cleave through even more mooks until they fall unconscious.

Deconstructed Once the hero calms down, they look back and see all of the lives they've taken, and the smell of the blood fills their nose as the guilt begins to swallow them up.

Reconstructed ...But their allies console them throughout it, telling them that so long as it doesn't happen again, and they can make up for the slaughter they had just committed, they'll be forgiven.

Averted The hero threatens to rampage throughout the entire mook HQ if they aren't given a precious safe. Buying the threat, two mooks roll the safe into the room to fulfill the order.

Lampshading "...What have you *done*? Are you supposed to be the hero here?"

Invoked The villain uses various means to make the hero more and more insane, then record the ensuing massacre in order to have everyone else root against the hero.

Beware the Nice Ones

Play it Straight	A polite, formal character will do their best to serve you with a smile, including fighting 4 mooks and defeating them with remarkable ease.
Downplayed	A polite, formal character is immensely patient with rude customers, but cross a line with them, and they'll reply with a seething remark while smiling.
Exaggerated	A near-saintly person is a friend to all, donates what they don't need to charity and *will* destroy you if you do something irredeemably evil.
Subverted	A polite, formal character will do their best to serve you with a smile, but when threats crop up, they're beat up before they can even strike.
Zig-Zag	...Which is fair, since they were caught off-guard. Now that they know the threat is there, they proceed to curbstomp all of their enemies immediately.
Deconstructed	The servant ends up bottling up a lot of anger, hate and other negative emotions, so when they eventually snap, they snap *hard,* and a lot of people are needed to stop them.
Reconstructed	...But when they are stopped, they're consoled, given some time off and allowed to relax a bit, letting them lower their formal walls a bit.
Averted	A polite, formal character who ends up running away from the very first threat, or a loudmouth "servant" who does their own thing and only helps out when heads need to be knocked in.
Lampshading	"Well what a surprise, my secretary who wouldn't slander a tyrant can take down 6 men and a tank alone."
Invoked	The servant needs to be more formal in their line of work, so they train themself to be such. When the gloves come off, they can resort back to their real self and beat people up.

Laser-Guided Karma

Play it Straight The villain manages to beat up the hero despite having their armies taken down. Before they can defeat the hero, one of the villain's slaves drives a large stake through their back, killing them.

Downplayed The villain manages to beat up the hero despite having their armies taken down. Before they can defeat the hero, one of the hero's allies grabs them out of the way while wounding the villain.

Exaggerated The villain manages to beat up the hero despite having their armies taken down. Before they can defeat the hero, a bolt of lighting strikes and evaporates the villain, who is weak to electricity.

Subverted The villain, with the hero at their feet, manages to defeat their nemesis after all this time, as they walk away freely.

Zig-Zag ...But the hero's greatest ally and friend runs to their corpse. Swearing revenge, they go on a rampage through the remaining mooks and defeat the villain alone.

Deconstructed The villain, deciding to change for the better is at the end of the road, and about to fully redeem themself when someone they previously wronged stabs them in the back.

Reconstructed ...Though through their good deeds and new friends, they're quickly saved from the wound and the assailant is warded off.

Averted The villain has the hero at their feet. As they prepare to deliver the finishing blow, lightning strikes behind them. Regardless, they stab the hero.

Lampshading "Wow, if I knew that was going to happen, I wouldn't have bothered coming all this way to beat you up."

Invoked A character can manipulate luck and probability, so they decrease the villain's luck/increase the probability that lightning will strike them.

O.O.C is Serious Business

Play it Straight A loud and rowdy character begins to act stiff, and remains silent unless spoken to. Turns out this is because of the villain blackmailing them, and they're trying to alert their allies without speaking.

Downplayed A loud and rowdy character begins to act stiff, and remains silent unless spoken to due to an illness affecting their mind and/or body.

Exaggerated The entire crew begins acting mechanical and matter-of-factly, due to having been replaced by machine replicas.

Subverted The loud and rowdy character is quiet due to being *physically* afflicted with a curse/spell/illness/etc, and they make up for the limitation with excessive snark and outlandish acts.

Zig-Zag ...Which also turns out to be symptoms of the curse/spell/illness/etc, and shortly after, the character is fully controlled by it and betrayed the crew.

Deconstructed No one really reacts to the changes exhibited by the character, deciding that they're either drunk, on drugs or simply in a poor mood.

Reconstructed ...But one of the crew members takes it seriously, and tries to communicate with the former loud 'n rowdy character to see what the issue is.

Averted A character uses a work-in-progress mind control beam, and uses it on the loud and rowdy character. Nothing happens.

Lampshading "Okay, it's kind of creeping me out how quiet she is."

Invoked The loud and rowdy character intentionally acts stiff and out of character to signal that something is terribly wrong.

Anti-Hero

Play it Straight	A rough, pragmatic hero that will resort to measures that no other hero would even try, because their threat is that much worse than themself.
Downplayed	The anti-hero will end up breaking the law and using practical means to bring the villain down, but they'll still attempt to do it as morally as possible.
Exaggerated	The anti-hero regularly shoots mooks to death, doesn't listen to any law if it benefits them not to, and outright makes the audience wonder *how* they're even the hero.
Subverted	The hero uses underhanded means to take down one villain, but doesn't go any further than that single instance.
Zig-Zag	...But more and more instances of the hero using these tactics go on, and eventually, they're on the bad side of the law.
Deconstructed	After killing several villains, slaughtering countless mooks and breaking the speed limit, the anti-hero is arrested.
Reconstructed	...But seeing the anti-hero's good work in their own light, they're busted out by another group to keep acting as a vigilante.
Averted	The villain tries to break the hero, telling them that the only way villainy will truly be stopped is in death. Despite saying this, the hero spares their life and has them taken in.
Lampshading	"So you're telling me that the guy who shot a bunch of guns for hire, blew up an entire warehouse and executed the villain on-air is the ***HERO?!***"
Invoked	The villain *forces* the hero into using underhanded and illegal means to succeed, so the media feels worse about the hero's efforts.

The Woobie (pronounced wuh-bee)

Play it Straight A beat down character, often small and/or harmless who's had a rough life, meant to garner sympathy from the audience due to their numerous woes, and issues they face because of them.

Downplayed A character who's been through a divorce, being attacked in an alley, and losing their job in one month, and is mentally exhausted as a result.

Exaggerated The woobie lost their entire family in a fire, got their arm chopped off by some gangsters, exists as a perpetual pariah to their workplace/school and only wishes for good things.

Subverted The character says how they've lost their family this month, and been robbed twice this week. It's a complete lie meant to grab attention, as another character points out.

Zig-Zag ...Which, it turns out, was the *actual* lie, and the woobie did lose their family/was robbed. The other character likely tried to downplay how the woobie is really feeling.

Deconstructed Due to their broken-down and seemingly passive nature, unsavory people may try and act friendly toward them in an attempt to benefit off of them, seeing them as an easier target.

Reconstructed ...Which fortunately falls short *because* of all that they've gone through, they can't trust anybody, and that includes the people trying to get close for personal gain.

Averted The hero asks a character if they're okay after all that they've been through, and they say yes. The hero and audience has no doubt about the response afterwards.

Lampshading "How do you pull through every day with what you've gone through, hugs or something?"

Invoked The villain inserts a mole into the hero's crew with the backstory and personality of a woobie, in hopes that the crew grows close to them. Odds are that this will backfire, and the mole will join the crew.

Nice Guy

Play it Straight	A genuinely kind-hearted, nice character who supports those around them. Not restricted to men, or humans for that matter.
Downplayed	The character is a little bitter, and may cause a few scenes here and there, but they're definitely going to pull through for those important to them.
Exaggerated	The character always pays the tab, opens the door for *everyone*, regardless of the situation and with the right information, could be a better therapist than the entire industry.
Subverted	A character acts polite and helps other people, but has a hair-trigger temper as well. As such, they're a lot more likely to scream your head off if you wrong them in any way.
Zig-Zag	...But again, that's just his temper, and he tries to work through it without letting it deter him in his efforts to make things better for everyone.
Deconstructed	Due to their nigh-selfless nature, people will often go to them for help with *everything*, on top of having the nice guy pay for all of their food, expenses, and more.
Reconstructed	...But they're actually that good at everything, and extremely rich as well. If not, they simply distance off from the leech in question while still helping those who need it.
Averted	The protagonist greets a receptionist, expecting someone polite or generally relaxed. What they get is an abrasive loudmouth who barely even does their job.
Lampshading	"Well, I don't think I needed the new car, or mansion, or buffet, or servants, or therapy session, but thanks I guess..."
Invoked	Seeing how cruel the world can be, the character decides to make themself the shining light of generosity and kindness in hopes that it will cause a ripple amongst people, making them do the same.

Evil Counterpart

Play it Straight	The villain to the hero, the big bad to the big good, and oftentimes the biggest threat the good side have to face. Expect it to be a fight on even footing when they clash.
Downplayed	While similar, the evil counterpart isn't a reflection of the hero/big good/crew, but they still serve to help the good side improve themselves in order to succeed.
Exaggerated	The evil counterpart is literally a mirror or alternate universe version of themself, who has become evil from whatever they went through.
Subverted	The hero encounters their evil counterpart, but it turns out to be a shadow of themself, with the same interests but different means. Essentially an anti-hero to a hero.
Zig-Zag	...Until the hero becomes too disturbed and mentally scarred from all they go through, which reflects on their shadow self, turning it into a monster.
Deconstructed	The evil counterpart sees how the hero gets everything, whereas they have nothing despite having more or less the same traits and powers. This causes them to hunt the hero down to replace them.
Reconstructed	...But noticing that they have some differences in common with the hero, they opt to be their true, darker self and realize that they *do* stand out, albeit in a bad manner.
Averted	The villain confronts the hero, talking about how similar they are, and how they're shadows to eachother. The hero then explains their life, traits and everything, disproving what the villain claimed.
Lampshading	"Wow, that is one *ugly* reflection you have there in the mirror."
Invoked	To give the unstoppable hero an actual threat, the villain projects all of the hero's vices into a different body with the same physique and powers to throw at the hero.

Affably Evil

Play it Straight A character is polite, even generous to others, but has an overarching goal that is undoubtedly nefarious in everyone's eyes.

Downplayed The villain is kind to their own troops, but overall, they intend to go through with their plan, even if that means sacrificing some men for it.

Exaggerated The villain teeters the line between a genuinely nice guy, and a world-ending threat at the same time. Expect them to throw parties and solve world hunger, while blowing the entire planet up afterwards.

Subverted The villain is kind, generous, and also planning on taking over the nation. Throughout the story however, that goal wavers, and eventually they betray their own cause to help the heroes.

Zig-Zag ...As a mole, with the heroes tied up, the villain serves them drinks and continues with the whole "national domination" thing.

Deconstructed The villain's behavior does nothing to sway how people see them, and they're treated horribly for their villainous actions, causing the affable element to slowly slip away.

Reconstructed ...But they decide that they're just not convincing people well enough, and recite their speeches a lot more in hopes that they'll sway people to their side better than before.

Averted The villain walks out with a smile, well dressed and acting upbeat. The second one of their troops makes a misstep, they explode into screaming, before shooting their troop dead.

Lampshading "Well if it weren't for that anti-hero being called an anti-**hero,** I would've thought that you were the good one!"

Invoked After some counseling and/or convincing. the villain becomes a nicer villain, but they can't simply let go of their goal mid-way through now.

Faux-Affably Evil

Play it Straight	The villain pays his troops well, treats his enemies respectfully, and... nope, he's horrible behind closed doors.
Downplayed	The villain tries to be nice, but the facade tends to crumble down anyway, so they're hardly bothered when it does.
Exaggerated	The villain walks in, celebrating their $1M milestone towards a charity, gives drinks to everyone on the house and proceeds to slowly saw an unlucky guest's head off for fun when they ask a question.
Subverted	The villain acts affable despite the horrible acts because that's the villain's personality. The faux comes from the perception of their actions.
Zig-Zag	...But those perceptions end up true, or becoming true once the villain has enough issues and breaks down into pure fury.
Deconstructed	The villain can't keep the act up forever, and people realize just how fake the "nice guy" front was this entire time, going against the villain afterwards.
Reconstructed	...But some people are fooled by it, and clash against those who doubt the villain, prompting a conflict between the two sides that the villain can use as a distraction.
Averted	The villain walks in, getting drinks for everyone on the house. A few characters talk about whether it's an act or not, to which the villain responds generously.
Lampshading	"Well that act could only stay up for so long."
Invoked	Being nice pays off, and it's a lot easier to do than making brainwash-rays or forcing people to work for you with power, so the villain decides to brush up on their charisma.

Hypocrite

Play it Straight	A character complains about their friend speaking too loudly, when they themself have no indoor voice whatsoever.
Downplayed	A character complains about their friend driving too fast, when they themself had gone well past the speed limit that one time months ago.
Exaggerated	A character complains about their friend eating too much after having one meal, when they themself have emptied the entire pantry of food from gorging down on it.
Subverted	A character complains about their friend driving too fast, when they themself had gone past the speed limit. Turns out, the speed limit had actually gone up, and they were going at a fair speed.
Zig-Zag	..."Oh not that, I mean the time before then," the hypocrite was (intentionally or not) referring to the time when they *hadn't* sped.
Deconstructed	While they are a hypocrite, they *do* have a point in what they're saying, and even moreso if they're making a conscious effort to change it whereas the other party isn't.
Reconstructed	...But the hypocrite has done the exact thing they're complaining about *far* more, and makes them seem even *more* hypocritical as a result if someone doing it *once* is enough to set them off.
Averted	The hypocrite nearly calls out their friend on how loudly they're speaking, only to realize how it would sound coming from themself.
Lampshading	"You can't complain about something that you're even *more* guilty of, you know."
Invoked	The hypocrite decides that he is *allowed* to speak loudly, due to being the leader, and anyone else just as loud needs to be quiet.

And I Must Scream

Play it Straight A character succumbs to a fate worse than death, whether eternal imprisonment or torture, or being used as fuel for some supernatural machine while still conscious of it.

Downplayed A character succumbs to a fate worse than death, whether imprisonment or torture, but their mind eventually dies, leaving them without a personality to suffer with.

Exaggerated A character is stuck in a time loop where they're tortured, killed, and rewound back to the start. Their mind is repaired every time, and the loop lasts for eternity, ensuring they never get out.

Subverted A character's mind is thrown into a device that simulates 1,000 years in the span of a second. After that, they're taken back into the world.

Zig-Zag ...Or so they thought. Their mind is still trapped in the device, and they're living in halluciations/ daydreams of their former world as a coping mechanism.

Deconstructed Due to being tossed into a device/room where 1,000 years passes in a second, they're either catatonic or completely feral afterwards, and die not long afterwards.

Reconstructed ...But through very extensive means, someone manages to essentially write a new personality over the catatonic person as a replica of themself. They're still mentally dead, but essentially "zombified."

Averted A character is thrown into an eternal prison that constantly heals them to keep them alive. It also heals the illness within them, which outperforms the body's immune system and killing the character.

Lampshading "Wow, that has to be one of the worst ways to go- no, even *going* is better than what you put them through."

Invoked The villain will unleash an unspeakable horror when they die, so to solve that, the heroes throw the villain into an eternal prison that keeps them alive and isolated from the world.

Moral Event Horizon

Play it Straight	The villain kickstarts their path to evil by burning the hero's village down after having a disagreement/ misinterpreting something the hero said.
Downplayed	The villain kickstarts their path to evil by kidnapping the hero's crush after having a disagreement/ misinterpreting something the hero said.
Exaggerated	The villain kickstarts their path to evil by starting an uprising, and destroying an entire city with armed forces because they had a crush on the hero's lover, who the villain kills as well.
Subverted	The villain burns down the hero's village, but it turns out that everyone there was being used as meat puppets by aliens.
Zig-Zag	...But they become delusional, and end up purging village after village of *innocent* people afterwards, prompting the hero and survivors to rise against the villain.
Deconstructed	Due to their actions being somewhat ambiguous, people believe that the villain accidentally started a fire, or that it was someone else altogether.
Reconstructed	...Which would've let them off, if they didn't try to start an uprising in order to hunt and bring in the hero afterwards.
Averted	The would-be villain comes close to throwing the torch in, but realizes how much they would lose if they did. They douse the torch, and pretend that nothing happened.
Lampshading	"Well, now you've crossed the line, and for what? Jealousy?"
Invoked	A bad mentor decides to test the would-be villain in an attempt to see how far they're willing to go for their selfish goals.

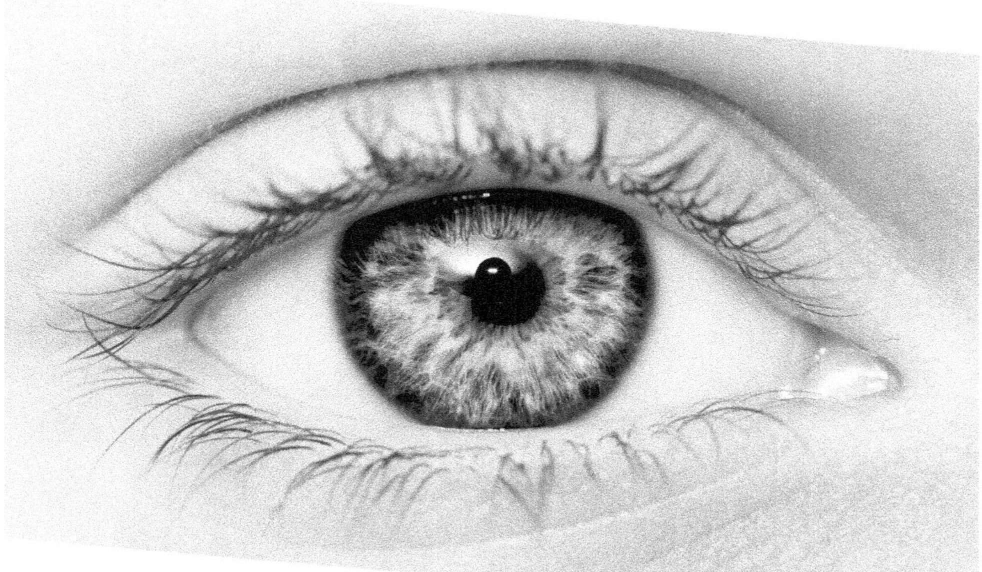

Eye Scream

Play it Straight	A sharp object collides with a character's eye, causing damage. The eye is one of the most precious bodyparts, letting us see the world and serving as a "window to the soul," so the result is life-altering.
Downplayed	A character is jabbed in the eye by another's finger. Aside from the initial fear, no real harm was done and the character in question is *real* mad.
Exaggerated	A character has both of their eyes ripped out with forks, leaving them completely blind. Even worse if they were known for their stunning eyes.
Subverted	A knife comes flying at the character's eye, only for it to clip their ear instead. Still painful and bloody, but their vision remains intact.
Zig-Zag	...Until another knife comes flying in, and lands straight in their eye, either killing them or rendering them unconscious.
Deconstructed	The eyes are the character's last concern, as the rapid blood loss from taking damage in such a vital location can end up killing them quickly.
Reconstructed	...But he's treated as quickly as possible, and while he's going to survive, his eyes may or may not have been repaired as well.
Averted	A crazed lunatic lunges to drive a fork through the character's eye, only for their ally to catch the assailant and beat them up.
Lampshading	"OW OWOWOWOW OW, ***AGH- AHHHH!***" followed by numerous instances of the character slamming surfaces.
Invoked	A monster is much less threatening if it can't see you, so the crew resorts to taking out its eyes in order to gain the upper hand.

Reasonable Authority Figure

Play it Straight An officer, manager, politician or anyone of high ranking who attempts to resolve everyone's issues in a reasonable manner.

Downplayed While not the best, the authority figure will put some effort into verifying whether their assistance is needed, and if so, come in with all they need to get it solved.

Exaggerated The second someone rings up the authority, he strolls in and resolves the problem immediately, whether a cat stuck in a tree, to aliens, to ending an entire war.

Subverted Once he rolls in, the authority tries to keep a grasp of the situation, only to be trampled on mid-way through.

Zig-Zag ...But later, he comes back to save the protagonist's friends after calling for backup. The day is saved, and the authority figure is essentially the story's hero.

Deconstructed Due to their helpful nature, the authority figure ends up checking out situations that aren't even problematic, wasting everyone's time in the process.

Reconstructed ...So they learn how to verify that their service is required in the first place. While this can backfire with legitimate cases, it helps weed out the phonies as well.

Averted The protagonist calls for help, due to aliens attacking their neighborhood. The person on the other end of the line scoffs, refuses and abruptly hangs up.

Lampshading "If we had more people like you with that kind of power, maybe the world would be a better place."

Invoked Due to the previous sheriff being horribly inept at their job, a new one is hired and thoroughly screened, then trained for the job in hopes that the county will be safe.

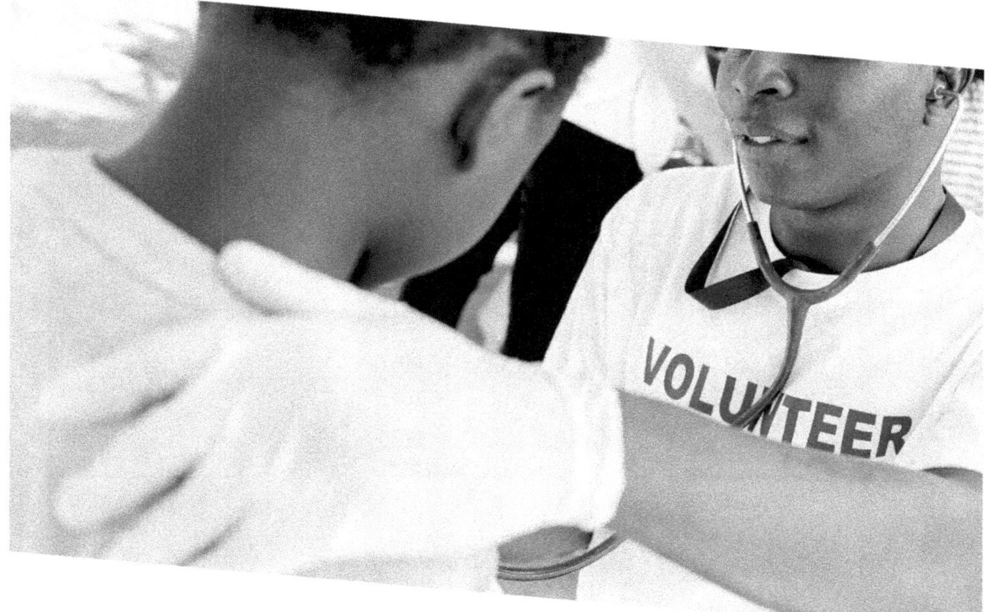

Establishing Character Moment

Play it Straight	A character enters the story by beating up a crook with a staff, nonlethally incapacitating them, and escorting the would-be victim out of harm's way. This shows that the character is a hero.
Downplayed	At a poker table, multiple characters are gambling for their lives. All but one are afraid, and the fearless one gets the highest hand, cluing the audience in on them having nerves of steel and great luck.
Exaggerated	Everything a character does in their introductory scene pretty much describes their entire character throughout the story.
Subverted	A character undergoes their establishing moment, only to be drastically different from how they were initially portrayed afterwards.
Zig-Zag	...But they do change, and gain those qualities seen when they first entered the story, whether intentionally or not.
Deconstructed	Due to the hero showing off so much about themself, down to the fighting style, M.O and limitations, the villains have a much better idea on how to handle them.
Reconstructed	...But regardless, the hero still succeed, maybe by switching up some weapons or simply improving themself with what they already have.
Averted	A character is introduced as a completely normal person. Not mysterious, not heroic, not any different from anyone else in the scene.
Lampshading	"I'm starting to expect a flashy banner to appear around you, saying who you are and what you do for a living."
Invoked	First impressions matter, and this character wants to make the most out of their debut, whether as a star, a hero or anything else where image matters.

Truth in Television

Play it Straight Something seemingly unrealistic in a work is actually plausible in reality, whether chemicals, psychology or location-wise.

Downplayed Something in the work has a resemblance to something that exists in real life, but to extremely impractical extents.

Exaggerated Something in the work is actually able to be applied in the real world. This only counts if it *seems* unrealistic, but is totally doable.

Subverted A car is examined, and all of the parts are according to their real-world counterparts, except for the engine running on plasma.

Zig-Zag ...But later on, as technology progresses in real life, that extremely abstract engine becomes a reality, and the work becomes truth in television, in hindsight.

Deconstructed Another one of the few tropes that can't be deconstructed (and therefor reconstructed,) though you can do a lot more with this than willing suspension of disbelief.

Reconstructed Another one of the few tropes that can't be deconstructed (and therefor reconstructed,) though you can do a lot more with this than willing suspension of disbelief.

Averted Everything within the work is extremely abstract, different anatomies, elements, societies and more, or everything in the work is very common knowledge in the real world.

Lampshading "Wait, you can actually do that?"

Invoked The author wants the audience to learn some abstract fun fact, while meshing it into the story that they're writing, as long as it fits in.

Arch-Enemy

Play it Straight Also known as a nemesis, the arch-enemy is oftentimes the main threat that the protagonist deals with, but can also be a rival that clashes with them from time to time. Not related to evil counterpart.

Downplayed While they aren't the protagonist's main enemy like the antagonist, they're definitely above the rest of the threats that the protagonist faces, and they may move on from the conflict altogether.

Exaggerated The arch-enemy is a bigger threat than the antagonist or big bad, and ends up being the one to nearly stomp the hero on every fight, wanting to kill the protagonist every time they meet.

Subverted The arch-enemy fights the hero and gives them a hard time, but eventually turns to support the hero, having gained respect for them throughout the story.

Zig-Zag ...But once all of the antagonists are out of the way, the arch-enemy draws their weapon on the hero once again, wanting to settle their feud without anyone else in the way.

Deconstructed The arch-enemy ends up being seen as a third party, or outright liability because of them dropping everything else to face the hero, so the villains may end up attacking the arch-enemy as well.

Reconstructed ...So the hero teams up with the arch-enemy, sets their differences aside and beats the villain tremendously faster than before with the both of them.

Averted The hero has to deal with the villain, the big bad and all of the empire, but none of them make it personal against them, since there's so many people rising up alongside the hero.

Lampshading "Okay, I'm seriously starting to wonder how you're *always* finding me wherever I go. My life doesn't revolve around fighting you, okay?!"

Invoked Determined to impede the hero, the villain digs up the hero's past and recruits the person who's likeliest to be their biggest enemy, convincing them into joining while arming them.

Despair Event Horizon

Play it Straight	Having missed a flight to a safer world, the character falls into despair, realizing they'll never make it out of the planet they're stranded on.
Downplayed	Having missed a flight to a safer world, the character feels hopeless due to being stranded on this awful planet, but they decide that they may as well try again regardless.
Exaggerated	The character misses a flight to a safer world, one that they've been wanting to go to for most of their life. They fall catatonic shortly after.
Subverted	The character misses a flight to a safer world. While they feel sad about it, they've grown used to their home planet anyway.
Zig-Zag	...Until they realized that their loved ones were on that ship, and now they're completely alone in a planet of death.
Deconstructed	Due to falling into despair, everyone around them sees them as the load, or simply dead weight, and end up refusing to help.
Reconstructed	...But one good person makes it their goal to help the despairing character through their sorrows and apathy.
Averted	A character misses a flight to a safer world, but they can't really be bothered about it. They still have friends and relatives where they are now, so it's alright.
Lampshading	"They haven't said a single word since they missed that flight. *Surely* they're fine, *right?*"
Invoked	To break the hero, the villain takes the hero's love interest, and launches them to the moon in a life support capsule, to be held there until the end of time. Bonus points if the hero is restrained.

The Mole

Play it Straight	A character acting on the behalf of one group, while being affiliated with another. Oftentimes reporting what happens to their true side, and the one who will open their enemy up for an attack.
Downplayed	A character passing through the HQ to do "repairs" ends up leaving some entrances for the villains to use in their attacks.
Exaggerated	The entire group is composed of moles working for other sides, and none of them know that the others are also moles.
Subverted	The one shady character of the group who keeps messaging strangers after attending group meetings is actually completely innocent.
Zig-Zag	...But of course, they were simply faking it, and they're even more likely to strike now that they were cornered.
Deconstructed	Due to the mole intending to blend in with the group, the very forces that they're assisting accidentally gun them down without noticing that they were the mole.
Reconstructed	...Good thing the mole packed an obvious outfit and kept it hidden from the group. If that's not an option, the mole simply gets out of there before the reinforcements can arrive.
Averted	The entire group is composed of childhood friends, trusted relatives and people who have truly dedicated themselves to their cause.
Lampshading	"Should've known you were the spy. All I can hope for now is that you didn't snitch on our lunch menu."
Invoked	Information is the greatest weapon. Knowing how many threats you're facing, the floor plan of the building and having an easy way in allows you to eradicate any threat with proper preparations.

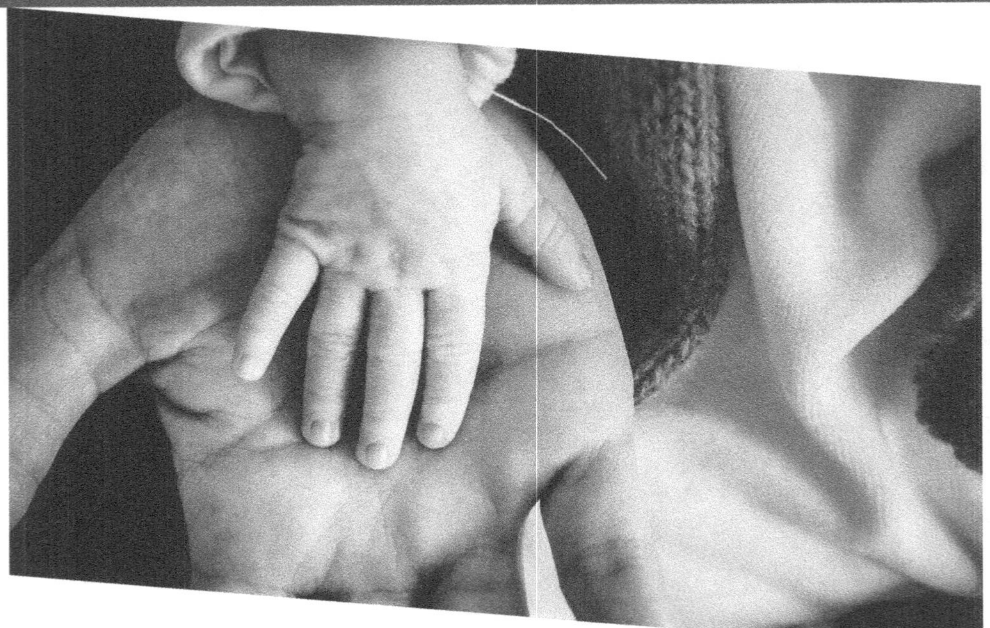

Papa Wolf

Play it Straight A fatherly figure who will fight tooth and nail for his children, or surrogate children. Strictly a male trope, with mama bear acting as the female counterpart.

Downplayed The father isn't the strongest, but he cares for the kids, and will put up a fight when they're threatened, even if it gets him killed.

Exaggerated The father, on hearing that a warlord tyrant who no one else can defeat has insulted his child, proceeds to curb stomp the tyrant in seconds.

Subverted All of the father's children say that he can easily beat up anyone who bullies them, but the fact is that he simply doesn't care.

Zig-Zag ...Until he sees them in real danger, which prompts him to jump into action, beating bad guys up left and right.

Deconstructed Due to the father taking so many matters into his own hands, his children may abuse that and get into trouble without any worries, until one of those issues ends up killing the father.

Reconstructed ...Or at the very least, wounding him. Scared for their father, the kids agree to stop taking his help for granted.

Averted After meeting a bunch of tough survivor kids, a character tries to meet their father, only to see a mama bear, or no parents whatsoever.

Lampshading "Wow, I feel like you're the kind of father everyone wishes they had."

Invoked After losing a child before, the father never wants to experience the pain, grief and attention that he felt from it, so he fights for every child.

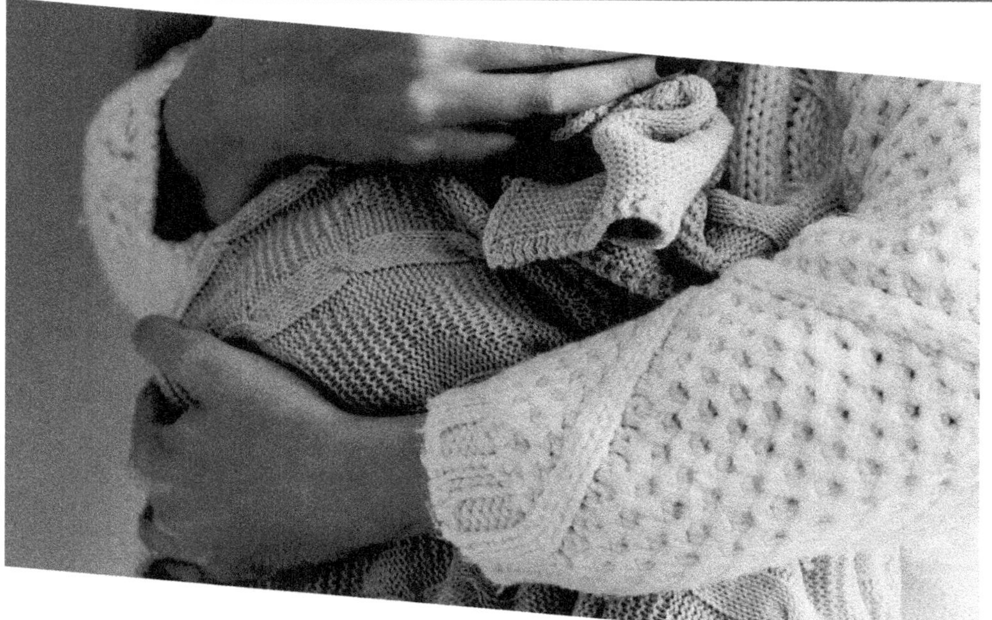

Mama Bear

Play it Straight	A mother who fights to keep her children safe, often preferring resourcefulness over brute strength like the papa wolf.
Downplayed	The mother will try her best to keep the kids safe, even if she doesn't know the best ways to do so, but regardless of her skill or resourcefulness, she'll make sure her kids make it out alive.
Exaggerated	The mother ends up beating everything that threatens her children with her bare hands, before completely burning down everything they hold dear. Or maybe something a little calmer.
Subverted	She has the air of a strong. protective mother, but if any threat arises, she ends up using her own children as bait to run away.
Zig-Zag	...So she could call for help. When that's done, she runs right back and attempts to take everyone somewhere safe until help arrives.
Deconstructed	Due to her efforts in keeping her children protected, she ends up sheltering them from the real world and all that comes with it, causing issues down the line.
Reconstructed	...But being told this, she makes an effort to let her children have some freedom, while being ready to help them when they need it.
Averted	After meeting a bunch of tough survivor kids, a character goes to their home to see that they only have one father, or no parents at all.
Lampshading	"Sheesh, I feel like she'd beat up the empire more than the hero can!"
Invoked	In a similar case to papa wolf, the mama bear lost a child early on, and takes a much more active, protective role in the lives of her future children.

Killed Off for Real

Play it Straight	A character's death is absolutely final, and they never come back for the rest of the story/series. This only applies if death is otherwise revertible.
Downplayed	A character's death is absolutely final, and they never come back through being revived, though their death *could* be prevented by going back in time.
Exaggerated	The character is killed in such an absurd way that even their memories, actions and existence are killed off with them.
Subverted	A character is killed off, but at the last minute, the crew finds out a way to reunite with them and bring them back to the mortal realm.
Zig-Zag	...Except they only revive the body. The personality, soul and mind are completely lost, and there's no getting those back.
Deconstructed	Due to their allies dying, the crew tries to find way after way to revive them in some form, but their efforts are a waste, and they end up overwhelmed by the empire due to spending their resources poorly.
Reconstructed	...But they manage to find a way to revive their allies, making death cheap as the full crew takes on the empire and wins.
Averted	The very-dead ultradoom beam is charged up and fired at a character, only for them to sidestep the beam and survive the blast.
Lampshading	"Yeah, he's not coming back from that one."
Invoked	Due to the villain being an unstoppable threat who can't stop coming back, the heroes make a way to completely eviscerate them, ensuring that their reign of terror ends with them.

Death is Cheap

Play it Straight A character dies, which would be tragic if it weren't for the fact that they'll be back next episode/chapter/entry in the series.

Downplayed While it takes some time, effort and money to put a character back together, it's totally doable, and in some places outright commonplace.

Exaggerated Characters die by the thousands each day, and outright test dangerous equipment without any safety gear due to reviving in perfect condition within the hour.

Subverted A character is blasted by the very-dead ultradoom beam, believing that they would come back from it. No points for guessing what happens.

Zig-Zag ...Except it was a knockoff very-dead ultradoom beam, and it didn't actually kill the character for real, they come back later no worse for wear.

Deconstructed People can still feel pain, and wars are waged with essentially infinite manpower, causing a lot of trauma that *can't* be healed through death. The world becomes a shell-shocked nightmare as a result.

Reconstructed ...Until people find a way to reverse death, *and* trauma. With this, the world becomes normal again, and the pointless wars cease altogether.

Averted A character is thrown off a rooftop, expecting to come back later like everyone else, but they stay dead for the rest of the series.

Lampshading "Wait, how many times have you died this week?"

Invoked Having enough people for your army/efforts is crucial, and what better a way to keep that number high in low-life expectancy roles than to revive them every time they die?

The Chessmaster

Play it Straight	A character plays the heroes, villains, big bad, big good and every variable into their desired outcome, through careful manipulation, setup and strategy.
Downplayed	The chessmaster plays some gangs into their own hands, using them to disrupt the hero, while also offering the hero some advice on how to beat them, for a favor later on...
Exaggerated	The chessmaster causes an uprising amongst pantheons, gods are beating eachother up and the world falls apart due to the chessmaster, a normal human, orchestrating the divine feud.
Subverted	The chessmaster plays both the villains and heroes against eachother, but ends up missing a detail that causes it all to crumble down.
Zig-Zag	...So their enemies are confident with the chessmaster dead, but they had already set up the rest of the plan to carry on without them, finishing perfectly at the end.
Deconstructed	The intelligence and foresight required to be an efficient chessmaster are extremely unrealistic, and most people who try end up having holes in their plans, resulting in immediate failure.
Reconstructed	...But one plays it straight, managing to account for every outcome, has the charisma to sway every side and manages to get what they want by the end.
Averted	The conflict of the story ends up being a pointless struggle between the heroes and villains, with absolutely no in-depth planning to go off of.
Lampshading	"Good prediction, accounting for my arrival. Guess you've also predicted my fist in your face?"
Invoked	Due to being sorely outnumbered and otherwise normal, the chessmaster needs to plan, plot and manipulate in order to get what they want, instead of pure power like the villains and heroes.

Smug Snake

Play it Straight A character who acts mightier than everyone else with a perpetual air of smugness around them. Generally not going to be liked by many people.

Downplayed A character who's prone to some smugness when they're having their way. Otherwise, they're prone to anything *but* smug when actual issues arise.

Exaggerated The smug snake's aura of smugness and arrogance can be felt in every scene that they're in, even making it something characters and the audience can *sense* before they're revealed.

Subverted The smug snake's aura is simply a facade, and they're actually really insecure about their own image, trying to use the "cool" smug persona to fit in.

Zig-Zag ...So they get used to it, and end up adopting the smug persona as their real self, essentially becoming the "fake" version of themself that they created to fit in.

Deconstructed Everyone quickly gets sick of hearing, seeing, and generally perceiving the smug snake in any form, causing them to be isolated.

Reconstructed ...But they were simply in the wrong crowd, and they find a much more acceptable (and likely just as smug) group of people to fit in with.

Averted A character decides to make a smug remark at the expense of a villain, only for their partner to elbow them in the gut. No further remarks occur in the story.

Lampshading "Ugh, the sleazy, "better than you" mentality this guy has is making me sick."

Invoked The villain wants to annoy the heroes as much as they can to provoke them into making mistakes.

Comically Missing the Point

Play it Straight A character walks in to order a drink of whiskey at a bar, not noticing the countless patrons of the bar brawling around them.

Downplayed A character walks into a chicken restaurant on Sunday. They wait, and wait, and wait, but no one serves them. It's only after 14 minutes that they realize the place is closed.

Exaggerated An entire group of friends go to said restaurant on Sunday, waiting and waiting until the employees arrive for work the very next day, seeing a broken door and customers waiting.

Subverted They did notice the brawl going on around them, but tried to ignore it in an attempt to be a less-obvious target, simply wanting their drink and nothing else.

Zig-Zag ...And after they get their drink, they walk out and have a knife pulled on them by a criminal. Instead of being afraid of it, they examine the knife and compliment it, to the criminal's confusion.

Deconstructed Due to their inability to get the point, they end up missing a crucial step in the plan, and the whole thing comes tumbling down shortly after.

Reconstructed ...Until they try and improvise, pulling through with dumb luck and quick wit despite having started the chaos in the first place.

Averted A character has a knife pulled on them in a robbery. They freeze, and hand over their belongings before attempting to run away.

Lampshading "So uh, that big flashing sign that usually says open? It *wasn't* flashing when you came in? You really shouldn't have to smash the front door open to enter a restaurant? What is *wrong* with you?!"

Invoked The character is feigning stupidity, so they pretend to miss what other people are saying/intending, in order to slack off or catch them off guard.

The Ace

Play it Straight A character who excels at physical, mental, charismatic, and technological matters (when applicable,) often being capable of operating in any role and often being the face of an operation.

Downplayed While not the best in any regard, the ace is still more than viable to fit into any role in the team, and works along with their allies really well.

Exaggerated A one-man army across the board, the most charismatic, technological eptitude, and physically tried character who can stomp every single obstacle in mere seconds. A modern factotum.

Subverted The ace carries the crew through countless operations, until they're mortally wounded, losing an arm in the process. Due to being out of action for so long with this, they lose an edge on their skills.

Zig-Zag ...But despite that, they have a replacement arm that functions just as well, if not better than their previous, and they hone their skills more in the meantime.

Deconstructed The ace ends up being the go-to character for anything that poses a threat, which taxes them extensively and ends up ruining the entire operation if they go down.

Reconstructed ...But then again, they're the *ace*, the strongest card, and they prove their worth by excelling at their tasks, while being perfectly fine with being sent on the harder tasks.

Averted The crew is composed of one heavy lifted, one charismatic leader, the smart guy and the sorcerer. None of them can really fit other roles, and they all work together to make up for their weaknesses.

Lampshading "I'd really hate to see how long your resume is, with all you do on a regular basis."

Invoked Wanting to be a factotum, the ace trains themself on countless topics, languages and physical training, while making an effort to soak up all that they learn and experience, so they're *always* improving.

Roaring Rampage of Revenge

Play it Straight A character loses a loved one, and proceeds to go on a complete rampage on their own, taking down tens to hundreds of enemies for the sake of revenge/avenging their loved one.

Downplayed A character loses their prized tropy, and enacts revenge on the one who broke it, and their friends as well, albeit in a non-lethal manner.

Exaggerated A character loses their loved one, home, and is treated as a pariah. Because of this, they singlehandedly destroy an entire country for revenge.

Subverted A character, in the height of their rampage, corners the one who wronged them, but they're suddenly beaten down and thrown off a bridge by another enemy.

Zig-Zag ...But they survive the fall, not broken and still vengeful for the blood of those who wronged them. They won't stop with being thrown off a bridge, they stop when their enemy is dead.

Deconstructed Due to their actions, bodies litter the streets, people are terrified everywhere and the rampaging character has no one to defend them when they inevitably go down.

Reconstructed ...But they keep persisting despite that, not needing anyone else due to them being a one-man army. They know that the rampage ends with their enemy's death, so the sooner the enemy dies, the less people die.

Averted The villain orders henchmen to kill off someone's wife and burns his home. Not wanting to have a potential threat, they also kill the would-be threat who was elsewhere when the house burnt down.

Lampshading "One person wronged you, and now the corpses of hundreds litter the streets!"

Invoked The villain really wants to break the hero, and have them fall to the same level. It's really easy to do, the villain kills the hero's loved ones and simply watches what happens afterwards,

Bad Boss

Play it Straight	A white collar boss is hated by all of their employees, they slack off while expecting the world of their workers and fire people over petty matters.
Downplayed	The boss is a bit lazy, unfriendly, and generally not the best leader by any means, but they aren't the worst boss you could be saddled with either.
Exaggerated	The boss fires you if you don't go through with their downright illegal requests, sets the employees up to fail and only lets those who stroke the boss' ego succeed in the workplace.
Subverted	The boss is barely even seen in the office, hardly guides their employees, and seemingly steals all of the coffee. When times get desperate however, they crawl out of their office and get people working good.
Zig-Zag	...Because they'd be fired, and they want the pay without much effort. After this instance, they slip back into the office, doing whatever they enjoy as their employees struggle outside.
Deconstructed	Due to the many things the boss has done wrong, they're reported to higher-ups or outright exposed on the news/internet by whistleblowers, causing them to quickly crumble.
Reconstructed	...But the company has taken a liking to the bad boss, and ends up covering up the numerous misdeeds to try and let the controversy die down.
Averted	The new employee, dreading her soon-to-be boss, strolls into the office and meets the boss, only to realize that they aren't that bad, and are outright reasonable.
Lampshading	"I swear, you would've been fired by now if you were the boss. In fact, if you had a clone of yourself working here, you'd fire yourself!"
Invoked	The boss intentionally makes everyone loath them in order to have a common enemy. With a common enemy, the co-workers begin to cooperate, and they blaze through what the boss tells them to.

Sanity Slippage

Play it Straight	A character begins to go through a series of horrible events, which corrodes their mental wellbeing until they're insane.
Downplayed	A character goes through numerous traumatic events, but gets through it without too many complications.
Exaggerated	A perfectly well-off character has a book dropped on their toe, causing them to froth at the mouth and scream about the stars multiplying in order to devour the universe.
Subverted	A character goes through countless traumatic events, and to the confusion of their allies, they appear to be no worse for wear.
Zig-Zag	...But they're definitely starting to crumple with all that they've been thrown into, and eventually they could break at any minute.
Deconstructed	Despite the character's growing madness, they're still sent off to handle dangerous tasks, which worsens their condition more and more until they break.
Reconstructed	...But they're given time off after they snap, and efforts are made to try and help them through their psychological scarring.
Averted	A character loses their family, home and job in one night, fights unimaginable horrors the next day and is completely fine with it all, somehow.
Lampshading	"Maybe you need some rest, your eyes look heavy all the time."
Invoked	The hero's a lot less trustworthy and ideal if they're a raving lunatic, so the villain tries their best to drive the hero absolutely insane in order to ruin their image.

Ascended Extra

Play it Straight A side character who gains enough traction with the audience and/or writer, that they become one of the crew, or even a main character of a spinoff.

Downplayed A side character or background character who gains enough of a following, that they become a recurring character within the work.

Exaggerated A character who became so adored by the audience, that they outright usurp the protagonist of their role and take over the story.

Subverted A character appears to be recurring, building relationships with the main cast, until they're suddenly killed off.

Zig-Zag ...But the crew makes an effort to try and undo the death. Time travel, revival magic or whatever else ensures that the ascended extra comes back for good, and maybe becomes one of the crew as well.

Deconstructed Due to the character's ascension into a lead role, they end up being thrown into the fray a lot more than before.

Reconstructed ...But they've gotten themself this far, so they quickly adapt to being one with the heroes, and manage to thrive in doing so.

Averted Throughout the series, none of the characters become more or less prevalent, the protagonist is still the protagonist, and the side characters are still side characters.

Lampshading "Guess I'm one of the big guys now, huh?"

Invoked The author notices how much traction a side character is getting, so instead of their original plan for the character, they instead promote the extra into a main character to appease the audience.

No-Sell

Play it Straight	A character is punched in the gut with enough force to kill a normal person, but it has no effect on the recipient.
Downplayed	A character is punched in the gut with enough force to kill a normal person, but it doesn't kill the recipient, only launching them back and wounding them.
Exaggerated	A character is punched with the power of a nuke, wiping out the entire country around them in the process. They take no damage, looking their assailant in the eye.
Subverted	A character is punched in the gut with enough force to kill a normal person, and when the character is punched, they're sent flying and nearly die as a result.
Zig-Zag	...But once they get up, they're punched again to no effect. They needed to take damage in order to build an immunity to it, which they now use against the assailant.
Deconstructed	Due to the character being un-phased by every attack, everyone decides to avoid dealing with them, and fight the other threats instead.
Reconstructed	...But the impervious character begins to dive into the assailants, using their own body to block would-be fatal attacks in order to save their allies.
Averted	A character is punched with enough force to kill a normal person, and despite them attempting to block the attack, they're launched back and immediately die.
Lampshading	"How on earth did you survive a *nuke?!* You're treating it like it was a bug bite!"
Invoked	To protect themself against the villain's killer venom, they inject themself with small doses of the villain's signature venom in order to build a tolerance for it.

Undying Loyalty

Play it Straight A character, animal, minion or summon fights for their master, no matter the circumstances, even if it means sacrificing themself to save their master.

Downplayed A character pledged their life to their master, and while they do want some free agency over their own lives, they will fight tooth and nail for their master.

Exaggerated A character essentially acts as an extension of their master's will, not even hearing what they're being told before doing it precisely as their master wishes.

Subverted The servant helps their master to the best of their ability, but eventually betrays them in favor of their enemy paying better.

Zig-Zag ...Which was a ploy to get behind their lines and tear them all apart. When the servant returns, expect some apologies.

Deconstructed Due to their loyalty, they may eventually become fanatical to their master, and obtain a sort of slave mentality towards them, doing whatever they deem at the costs of the servant's wellbeing.

Reconstructed ...But their master is fair, and ensures that the servant gets enough time to be themself, since the master can handle matters on their own as well.

Averted Every single one of the master's servants ends up betraying them, slacking off, or overriding whatever the master wishes.

Lampshading "I wouldn't be too surprised if you served as that woman's footstool."

Invoked An unsavory master may use brainwashing, blackmail or various other means to make their servant do everything that the master wishes for.

Wham Episode

Play it Straight	An episode, chapter or arc that completely flips the story thus far on its head, revealing something about a character that the characters and audience have experienced in another light.
Downplayed	The ending of an episode, chapter or arc reveals that two of the crewmembers are actually relatives, but this is less surprising to the audience if we picked up on the clues beforehand.
Exaggerated	The ending of an episode, chapter or arc that reveals that the entire story thus far has been a dream, or the protagonist's delusions.
Subverted	Near the end of the episode, chapter or arc, the antagonist almost reveals that they're relatives to the protagonist, but they are struck down before they can say it.
Zig-Zag	...But on examining the corpse, the protagonist finds an old picture of the antagonist and protagonist when they were young, realizing who they were the whole time.
Deconstructed	The protagonist doesn't feel too conflicted by this revelation though, because they didn't really grow up alongside their antagonistic sibling enough to build a bond with them.
Reconstructed	...But they do start to feel a bit guilty, and they can't quite get it out of their mind. Expect the protagonist to slowly spiral out of control until they're confronted about their feelings.
Averted	Near the end of the episode, chapter or arc, the antagonist tries to stall for time by "revealing" pointless things that the crew already knew. Tired of the antagonist's stalling, they strike the villain down.
Lampshading	"I swear, why do these people always save such important details near the end!"
Invoked	The antagonist was torn on whether or not they should tell their secret to the hero, but being put on death's door has given them the courage to.

Break the Cutie

Play it Straight A character, typically younger, ends up going through numerous horrible situations that breaks their spirit, and hardens them for the rest of the story.

Downplayed An innocent character is lost, gets a little roughed up and is generally a mess until they're found, and brought home safely.

Exaggerated The character is already a woobie by this point, but in spite of that, they're still beaten on a daily basis, starved, doing the worst jobs known to man and finally killed off once they stop crying.

Subverted An innocent character is tossed into an alleyway full of crooks, thieves and other criminals. Instead of being robbed of everything valuable, they're treated to a criminal wonderland that acts as a safe-zone.

Zig-Zag ...Until they're lured out, in which they're stabbed in the back, robbed, and hauled off to some dumpster that they later crawl out of in an attempt to get help.

Deconstructed Due to the constant fear of this happening, even in real life, parents will keep an eye on their children to ensure that nothing bad happens to them, and they don't see the cruel reality of the world.

Reconstructed ...Which is still pointless, because the teen still manages to sneak out, and ends up getting robbed on their first solo outing.

Averted The character drifts away from their group of trustworthy friends, and nearly walks into a dangerous alleyway only to be stopped by one of those friends.

Lampshading "Yeah, sure sounds like you weren't one of the lucky ones growing up."

Invoked An extremely strict parent may let their teen go off free, locking them out and forcing them into the world that they want to be free in, just to show them how dangerous it is out there. Various bad things happen to the youth, and the parent uses those awful things that happened to the youth against them.

The Atoner

Play it Straight A character has done something in the past, and acts to atone for it in the present, whether by fixing their mistakes as directly as they can, or doing an equal amount of good to offset the bad.

Downplayed While they do feel guilt for their past actions, the atoner tries to make up for it in either a single large action, or smaller actions that lack consequences.

Exaggerated The second an atoner accidentally steps on a cat's tail, they stomp on their own foot to atone for their heinous crime against feline-kind.

Subverted While the atoner declares that they will set things straight after their roaring rampage of revenge, they get pretty much nowhere, and instead slack off.

Zig-Zag ...But they were really preparing themself for the task at hand, and they begin to right the numerous wrongs that they had committed in the past.

Deconstructed Despite their attempts to atone for all of their bad deeds, no one else sees the good that they've done as sufficient compensation, if anything at all, and still hates the atoner for all the bad that they're known for.

Reconstructed ...But after the atoner nearly sacrifices themself for the people when a villain nearly nukes the country, they all forgive the atoner, and help them back on their feet.

Averted A character goes through a roaring rampage of revenge, slaughtering countless people before killing their target. Once that's done, they continue with their life like nothing happened.

Lampshading "I go to sleep each night, praying that every body I keep above ground makes up for those I had buried in my fury."

Invoked While otherwise unbothered, society, a sworn oath or their own personal code deems that they must make up for all the bad they do, with good deeds.

Put on a Bus

Play it Straight	A character takes a trip elsewhere, whether mentioned or not, and doesn't appear for the rest of the story, unless the bus comes back.
Downplayed	A character takes a break, and they don't appear for a few chapters/scenes whatsoever, until they're called back into action.
Exaggerated	A character seen in the beginning doesn't appear for the rest of the story, and their disappearance isn't explained at all.
Subverted	A character decides to take a trip elsewhere, but comes back to help the protagonist after having forgotten their belongings for the trip.
Zig-Zag	...So after that, they pack up all their stuff, and take the trip for real, either retiring or coming back at a later scene.
Deconstructed	Due to their vacation, they end up missing an assault on the crew's HQ, and had they been with the crew, everyone would've survived.
Reconstructed	...But the crew handles the situation themselves, not wanting to worry the one on vacation with the HQ assault, so they clean everything up and carry on like usual.
Averted	A character has a ticket to another country, but when something crops up, they decide to stay and help the crew out with it.
Lampshading	"Oh, tomorrow's my trip. I hope all of you can handle yourselves without me for a few weeks."
Invoked	The villain intentionally sways one of the crewmembers to take a vacation in order to take over the HQ easier.

The Bus Came Back

Play it Straight A character who was put on the bus comes has finally come back from their trip, and they're ready to get back into action.

Downplayed A character who was put on the bus is back for a little while, mainly to help with whatever the matter is, but once that's handled, they go right back to where they came from.

Exaggerated A character who was put on the bus suddenly teleports in when the heroes are about to be defeated, to surprise the villain (and heroes) with a kick to the face.

Subverted A character comes back, and greets the rest of the crew, only to immediately go on another trip the very next day.

Zig-Zag ...Except for the crew "convincing" them to stay. Begrudgingly, they decide against another trip until they've put enough time in with the crew to justify it.

Deconstructed When they finally get back, they're yelled at by the crew for leaving *right* as the villain launched an attack on their HQ, before calling them a mole for the convenient timing.

Reconstructed ...But the crew eventually calms down, and tries to assure the character that they're simply concerned with the coincidence, and the character handing some souvenirs to the crew helps lighten the mood.

Averted The crew eagerly waits for the character to return from their vacation, only to hear that the plane they took crashed.

Lampshading "Alright guys, I am back- *uh, what all did I miss?...*"

Invoked The crew quickly calls the character off of their vacation when their HQ is under attack, prompting them to return home immediately.

Book Ends

Play it Straight The story starts with a sunrise, the protagonist waking up, and the smell of pancakes lingering through the air, and ends with the protagonist going to sleep at sunset, with the smell of pancakes in the air.

Downplayed The story starts with the protagonist waking up to a sunrise, and ends with them slowly dying, looking at a beautiful sunrise.

Exaggerated The story starts with the character driving to work as a jazzy tune plays on the radio. At the end, the hero warps back in time and that very scene repeats, ending the story there.

Subverted The story starts with a sunrise and the protagonist waking up to the smell of pancakes. The story ends at the same location, but forgoes the sunrise and pancakes.

Zig-Zag ...Only to cut to the protagonist waking up at sunrise, smelling the aroma of pancakes in the air, before the story ends.

Deconstructed The story ends the very way it started, showing how little the protagonist has truly changed throughout their journey.

Reconstructed ...But something happens shortly after they wake up, showing them handling things a lot better than before, proving that yes, they have changed, and they will keep changing for the better.

Averted The story starts with a sunrise and the protagonist waking up to the smell of pancakes, but it ends with the protagonist on their knees, before passing out in broad daylight.

Lampshading "Well, back to square one. At least I have a better idea of where to go from here."

Invoked Trying to welcome the protagonist back into a normal life, their love interest cooks them pancakes before they wake up for that morning fragrance.

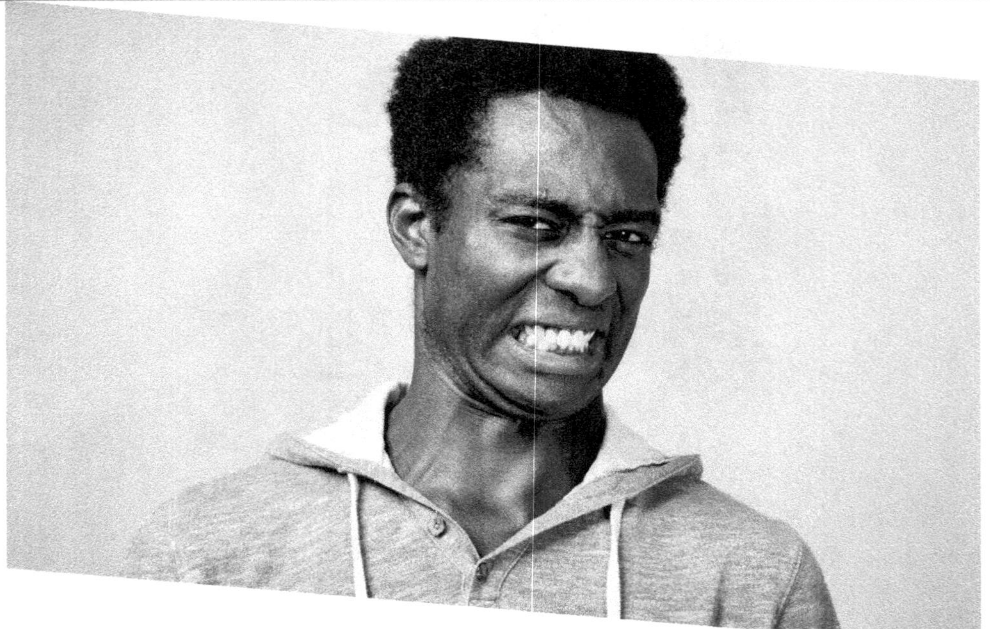

Groin Attack

Play it Straight A character shoots, stabs or slams a weapon into another character's groin to keep them stunned long enough for an easy finisher.

Downplayed A character kicks or knees another in the groin, whether for a "prank," annoyance or out of spite towards them.

Exaggerated The character takes down *every* enemy with one of these, often building up a terrifying reputation for doing so.

Subverted A character delivers a kick seemingly aimed for the groin, only for the would-be target to block the kick or dodge out of the way.

Zig-Zag ...So the character delivers a leg sweep to their target, knocking them to the ground and finishing with a follow-up stomp on the groin. Really putting some work in for such a low-blow.

Deconstructed Their opponent is wearing a cup, or has an immense pain tolerance that causes them to no-sell the kick, often to the kicker's surprise.

Reconstructed ...So the character instead opts for outright weaponry, staggering the opponent with various blows before slamming a sledgehammer into their groin.

Averted For those who want to stop imagining the terror and pain that this would bring, here's your break. The character never uses such low-blows due to fighting honorably.

Lampshading "HOW COULD YOU DO THAT?! COME ON, YOU NEED TO HAVE SOME DIGNITY!"

Invoked Everywhere else is heavily guarded, so to the opponent's misfortune, the character has only one place to strike.

Punny Name

Play it Straight A character has an awful "punny" name, often causing excessive groaning and exhaustion of anyone who hears it.

Downplayed A character has an alias with a tongue-in-cheek pun to try and make others laugh, often with little to no success.

Exaggerated Puncle Frye walks into his nephew's birthday party, serving a platter of french fries while making absolutely atrocious puns on fries.

Subverted Other characters mention a friend of theirs having a funny name, but when they're met for the first time, the name seems entirely normal.

Zig-Zag ...Until they read the character's full name, Christopher Hector Ian Le Dane, and see the acronym with the full name.

Deconstructed The pun often goes over peoples' heads sicne the character doesn't mention their full name, often out of embarrassment from seeing others reacting to it.

Reconstructed ...But the few times that they do tell people their full name, it goes over well to their surprise, and encourages them to use it more often.

Averted A character jokes about how their name is a totally abstract pun, and they try to explain it, only for it to clearly be senseless rambling.

Lampshading "I honestly feel bad for you if you grew up with a name like that."

Invoked One parent makes a joke about naming their child with a pun, and the other parent without a sense of humor, agrees to it.

Never My Fault

Play it Straight	The villain ends up demolishing two bridges to the city, and wiping out the power lines before claiming that it wasn't their fault, it was the city council's.
Downplayed	The villain wipes out the city's power lines, and claims that the heroes attacking them made them resort to such an extreme measure.
Exaggerated	The villain wipes out half of the planet, runs through the world's resources in weeks and proceeds to blame it all on the heroes, masses, their own troops, and even divine beings.
Subverted	The villain blows up every single bridge that leads in and out of the city, and actually begins to admit to having done it.
Zig-Zag	...*Because* of the hero, and the government, and the council, and their hallucinations, and God, and the illuminati, and other nations, and...
Deconstructed	Due to the villain never owning up to their mistakes, everyone else despises them, causing them to hardly gain any traction as a result.
Reconstructed	...But they end up coming back from this by framing the heroes in an incident involving multiple bridges blowing up, and with the fabricated proof, they declare once again, it wasn't their fault.
Averted	The villain blows up every bridge leading to a city, and wipes out the power grid for good measure, admitting to it while swirling their mustache.
Lampshading	"Well what *is* your fault then?!"
Invoked	The villain attempts to use this in order to deflect all of their actions onto others in an attempt to worsen their reputations, to varying degrees of success.

Breaking the Fourth Wall

Play it Straight A character looks at a massive pit with no bottom, then looks at the viewer/addresses the reader, saying that they sure aren't going down there.

Downplayed A character looks at a massive pit with no bottom, then says "if this were like one of my books/shows, then this pit likely has the treasure."

Exaggerated The story has no fourth wall, and the reader/viewer is constantly addressed by the characters. Expect boatloads of lampshading and jabs at the audience.

Subverted A character looks at a massive pit with no bottom, then says surely the treasure has to be down there, before looking at the viewer. Turns out, they were looking at someone pointing a gun at them.

Zig-Zag ...Then they jump down, landing somewhat safely as they address the reader, saying that they're glad they landed in one piece.

Deconstructed The characters' animosity begins to simmer up as the reader/viewer is simply watching the characters' suffering, and for enjoyment at that.

Reconstructed ...But they get over it, concluding that it must be better than *whatever world* the audience is stuck in, because they're adventuring, and the audience is flipping through a book/sitting and watching.

Averted The story keeps the willing suspension of disbelief going strong, and refuses to break the fourth wall for any gag.

Lampshading "Yes, I'm lampshading a fourth-wall break, which means I'm breaking the fourth wall while talking about breaking the fourth wall. Go figure, but on another note, go check back to page 32."

Invoked The writer wants to make a joke that mocks or teases the reader/viewer themself, and what better a way than to have a character make the joke at the audience's expense?

True Companions

Play it Straight	A band of characters who will fight tooth and nail for eachother, like a tight-knit family who revolves around adventure, romance, and everything in between.
Downplayed	While they aren't the most tight-knit group, they trust eachother to set their differences aside and fight together when times are dire.
Exaggerated	The companions are essentially a hivemind that constantly finish each others' lines, and fight so uniformly that they come across as a single person more than a group.
Subverted	The band of true companions fight and stay by each others' side, until one of them ends up clashing with the rest of the group.
Zig-Zag	...But it was really the villain in disguise. The group defeats the villain, and rescues their missing ally from an execution.
Deconstructed	Eventually, as people continuously change, their goals and ideals change with them, so the group ends up straying away.
Reconstructed	...But when times get dire, they return, remember their initial oaths to each other, and arm up for the grand battle.
Averted	A character is invited into a group of tight-knit oath-bound swashbucklers, but they refuse the call, not having trust in anyone else.
Lampshading	"Well look at us, the 6- er, 7 swashbucklers!"
Invoked	The fabled relic requires a group of 7 people, all with unwavering ideals to activate it. The heroes decide to fill up the ranks and become the ideal group for the task.

Must Have Caffeine

Play it Straight A character begins to chug down coffee, tea, or energy drinks the moment they feel tired in order to pick themself up.

Downplayed While they aren't a real coffee drinker, the character grabs a sweetened cup to pull through a particularly demanding task.

Exaggerated The character brews a new cup of black coffee the second the smell of the last cup has subsided, and runs off of enough caffeine to give any normal person a heart attack or two.

Subverted A person confidently walks into a coffeehouse, ordering a cup of coffee. As they take a drink, their face contorts into multiple dimensions from the bitterness.

Zig-Zag ...Turns out, they enjoy sweetened coffee, and the barista never asked if they wanted it sweetened, assuming it was supposed to be black.

Deconstructed Due to the constant consumption of coffee, the character's heart begins to get wonky, and they can even slip into a cardiac arrest from too much caffeine.

Reconstructed ...So they opt for dark roasts and brews with less caffeine, while limiting their intake to healthier standards in order to prevent future incidents.

Averted The character absolutely despises coffee, cherishing tea and committing *teason* as they sip their silly little plant water as opposed to the glorious bitter bean water.

Lampshading "Come on, you know I need 6 espressos to function here, right?..."

Invoked A character has a *really* extensive list of things to do, so they start chugging down coffee with reckless abandon in hopes that it'll help them pull through all their work.

Also From TLM Publishing House

FICTION:

Sydney Brown Presents Series

https://www.amazon.com/dp/B0BSBT36HN

The Mall Cadet Series

https://www.amazon.com/gp/product/B0B66MDK3T

All In or Nothing Series

https://www.amazon.com/dp/B0B7FW9W8M

The 7 Wishes Series

https://www.amazon.com/dp/B0B62XJY59

The Deception Series

https://www.amazon.com/dp/B0B5RNQMF1

The Forbidden Love Series (18+)

https://www.amazon.com/dp/B0B5SX24SX

NONFICTION:

How to Start It Series

https://www.amazon.com/dp/B09Y2QHDPM

Ready to share your story with the world?

I'm the writer publishing professional certification program that will teach you how to craft a fiction story so you can become a ghostwriter, or share your own stories with the world.

For more info, go to https://www.writercertification.com

www.ingramcontent.com/pod-product-compliance
Lightning Source LLC
Chambersburg PA
CBHW080207300326
41934CB00038B/3395
* 9 7 8 1 9 5 9 9 4 8 1 1 7 *